LATIN AMERICAN DANCING

Margaret Cantell L.I.S.T.D.

and

Paul Clements

TEACH YOURSELF BOOKS

For UK orders: please contact Bookpoint Ltd, 78 Milton Park, Abingdon, Oxon
OX14 4TD. Telephone: (44) 01235 400414, Fax: (44) 01235 400454. Lines are open from
9.00–6.00, Monday to Saturday, with a 24-hour message answering service.
Email address: orders@bookpoint.co.uk

For USA & Canada orders: please contact NTC/Contemporary Publishing, 4255 West
Touhy Avenue, Lincolnwood, Illinois 60646–1975, USA Telephone: (847) 679 5500,
Fax: (847) 679 2494.

Long renowned as the authoritative source for self-guided learning – with more than 40
million copies sold worldwide – the *Teach Yourself* series includes over 200 titles in the
fields of languages, crafts, hobbies, business and education.

A catalogue record for this title is available from The British Library.

Library of Congress Catalog Card Number: On file

First published in UK 2000 by Hodder Headline Plc, 338 Euston Road, London, NW1 3BH.

First published in US 2000 by NTC/Contemporary Publishing, 4255 West Touhy Avenue,
Lincolnwood (Chicago), Illinois 60646–1975 U.S.A.

The 'Teach Yourself' name and logo are registered trade marks of Hodder & Stoughton Ltd.

Cover photo from Dee Conway
Typeset by Transet Limited, Coventry, England.
Printed in Great Britain for Hodder & Stoughton Educational, a division of Hodder
Headline Plc, 338 Euston Road, London NW1 3BH by Cox & Wyman Ltd, Reading,
Berkshire.

Impression number   10 9 8 7 6 5 4 3 2 1
Year   2005 2004 2003 2002 2001 2000

CONTENTS

ACKNOWLEDGEMENTS

I have consulted ISTD Techniques material and many published works but should like to acknowledge my special indebtedness to the Latin section of *Teach Yourself Ballroom Dancing* (Hodder & Stoughton), and to its authors Peggy Spencer MBE and Gwenethe Walshe, and to my sister Jean.

MC

'Hell's Pavement' by John Masefield is reproduced courtesy of The Society of Authors as the literary representative of the Estate of John Masefield.

INTRODUCTION

This book is a between-class practice aid which makes use of some new ideas to speed up your progress. It describes 86 figures in ten Latin dances in language that beginners can understand. Any technical terms, which dance teachers sometimes use, are explained at the end of this Introduction or when they are introduced.

To make learning simple, we have incorporated three features which add realism to the dance chapters and make each of them seem more like an extension of a dancing lesson than a chapter in a text book.

■ We have given you and your partner separate pages because you have different steps;

■ The instructions for each step in each figure are printed on a half-tone band which represents a beat of music. These beat bands go from the top of the page to the bottom without breaks, because there are no breaks in the music. By revealing the rhythm and emphasizing the first beat in each bar of music, they show how your steps are tied to the music. They also make it easier to know when you should step off;

■ On the page facing the step instructions there are step diagrams in which each footprint is keyed to its instruction. Each diagram gives you a clear picture of the pattern of each figure and shows how you progress round the floor in the dances which travel. It also provides a numbered bird's-eye view of each new dance position that you and your partner adopt.

Every dance chapter is introduced by two pages devoted to the dance's origins, its music and mood. At the end of each chapter, after the figure instructions for men and for women, there are suggestions for perfecting your technique and notes on choreography.

How to use the book

First, become familiar with the last two pages of this Introduction – the dancing compass and the abbreviations and signs used in all the subsequent chapters. Next look at the first chapter, **Dance Positions**, and note which apply to the dances you are learning. You will see that there are two views of each position – full-length and bird's-eye.

The appropriate full-length, normal hold illustration is reproduced on the first page of each dance chapter. Whenever you move into another position, you will find a miniature bird's-eye view of it in the relevant step diagram.

To refresh your recollection of a figure (or to find out something about a new figure you are going to learn in class) first read the two pages which introduce the dance and then turn to the pages (Man's or Woman's) which describe your steps.

Note that the instructions for each step are printed on a half-tone music-beat band and identified by a number which is repeated by the relevant footprint in the diagram on the opposite page. Read through the instructions for each step of the figure and then follow the footprints (the left foot's prints are shaded) and note any bird's-eye hold position in the diagram.

If you have already danced the figure, put the book down and practise the steps with or without your partner. Add music if you can. It makes practising much more enjoyable and your teacher will recommend appropriate strict-tempo recordings.

Finally, when you know the steps, read the last two pages of the dance chapter and practise the figure again, concentrating on technique. There is much more to dancing than just taking steps. You should aim to perfect one figure before starting the next.

The dancing compass

The arrows on the dancing compass indicate where your feet are pointing in relation to the *line of dance* – the anti-clockwise path around the dance floor which couples follow when they are dancing travelling dances. The travelling dances in this book are the Samba, the Bossa Nova (sometimes), the Merengue (sometimes) and the Argentine Tango.

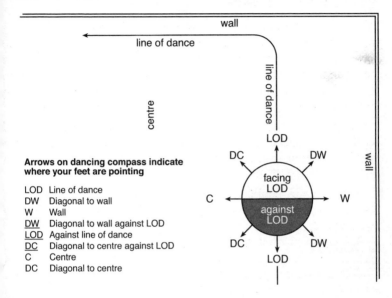

The dancing compass

Abbreviations

CBMP	Contrary body movement position	LOD	Line of dance
		LSP	Left side position
CPP	Counter promenade position	OP	Outside partner
		PP	Promenade position
DC	Diagonally to centre	Q	Quick
DH	Double hold	RF	Right foot
DW	Diagonally to wall	RH	Right hand
LF	Left foot	RSP	Right side position
LH	Left hand	S	Slow

Symbols used in foot diagrams and step instructions

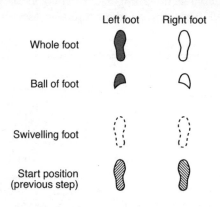

	Left foot	Right foot
Whole foot		
Ball of foot		
Swivelling foot		
Start position (previous step)		

S   Slow – a step taken over two beats

Q   Quick – a contrasting quick step

Bird's-eye views of dance positions

The shaded outline represents the Man. The solid outline represents the Woman.

  LSP (left side position) showing the Woman on the Man's left side.

  RSP (right side position) showing the Woman on the Man's right side.

1 | DANCE POSITIONS

Full length and bird's-eye views of twenty dance positions are shown in this chapter, five of which are normal hold positions.

A full-length view of the appropriate normal hold position is reproduced at the beginning of each dance chapter. Whenever you move into another position, you will find a miniature version of the bird's-eye view of it in the relevant step diagram.

    1 Normal hold used in the Cha-cha-cha, Rumba, Samba, Bossa Nova, Merengue and (optionally) Salsa.

    2 Normal hold used in the Mambo.

3 Normal hold used in the Salsa.

4 Normal hold used in the Jive and Rock 'n' Roll.

5 Normal hold used in the Argentine Tango.

6 Open facing position (one-hand hold) used in each dance except the Argentine Tango.

7 Handshake hold used in the Jive and Rock 'n' Roll.

8 Double hold (DH) used in each dance except the Argentine Tango and Salsa.

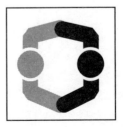

9 Double hold (DH) used in the Mambo, Merengue and Salsa.

10 (Man's) left side position (LSP) used in each dance except the Argentine Tango (moving forward).

11 (Man's) right side position (RSP) used in each dance except the Argentine Tango (moving back).

 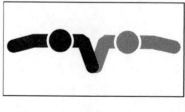

12 Promenade position (PP) used in each dance (moving forward).

13 Fallaway position used in the Mambo, Merengue, Jive and Rock 'n' Roll (moving back).

14 Counter promenade position (CPP) used in the Samba and the Argentine Tango.

The bar shows where you are looking.

15 Fan position used in the Cha-cha-cha and Rumba.

16 Alemana used in the Cha-cha-cha (step 5) and Rumba (step 3).

17 Hockey Stick used in the Cha-cha-cha (step 5) and Rumba (step 3).

18 Outside partner (OP) used in the Cha-cha-cha and Rumba.

The arrow indicates you should step on the right or left side of your partner and the direction of travel.

19 Outside partner (OP) used in the Argentine Tango.

The arrow indicates you should step on the right or left side of your partner and the direction of travel.

20 Spot Turn/Spot Volta used in the Cha-cha-cha, Rumba, Mambo, Samba, Bossa Nova and Merengue showing step 2.

2 | CHA-CHA-CHA

The Cha-cha-cha, perhaps the most popular Latin American dance, originated in Cuba where it developed from the quicker Mambo. Its tempo (30–34 bars per minute) is fairly quick. Its music, in 4/4 time (four beats to each bar) has an emphatic bongo drums' beat which is overlaid by the lighter tone of maracas so that each bar seems to say *cha-cha-**cha*** (two beats) *step-step* (two beats). Into these four beats five steps are squeezed.

Unlike ballroom dancers, who glide smoothly round the floor, couples dancing the Cha-cha-cha stay more or less in one place – taking small firm *ball flat* steps with abrupt changes of direction while responding with hip and leg movements to the rhythm of the music.

Chassés

The dance is a series of three-step chassés, each of them squeezed into two beats of music and connected by two linking, rocking steps. In most figures the *cha-cha-**cha*** (*half-beat half-beat-**beat***) chassé is danced moving sideways, but it may be danced on the spot or while turning or while travelling forwards or backwards. However the chassés are danced, your weight must be transferred as you take each step and held slightly longer on the last step.

The Basic Movement on pages 14 (man) and 22 (woman) has a forward and a backward half. Practise it until you can dance it with ease. It is the foundation on which all other figures rest.

Holds

Start facing your partner, about six inches (150 mm) away, in an upright position with your head erect. The man's right hand should be placed on the woman's left shoulder blade while her left arm is laid on his right, with her hand resting on his shoulder. Joined hands should be held lightly and raised to the man's eye level providing he is not a lot taller than his partner. This is called *normal hold* but, in Latin dances, your position in relation to your partner changes frequently. Some figures are danced with both hands held (*double hold*) some with one hand held (*one hand hold*) and some without hold.

Footwork

Footwork to be ball flat unless instructed otherwise.

Figure 2.1   Normal hold position

STEPS	**THE BASIC MOVEMENT**		BEATS
Start position (feet not illustrated). Normal hold. Feet apart.			
Weight on RF.			*One
	(forward half)		
1	LF forward		Two
2	Transfer weight back onto RF		Three
3	LF to the side	Cha	Four
4	Close RF halfway to LF	Cha	and
5	LF a small step to the side	**Cha**	*One
----------------(backward half)---			
6	RF back		Two
7	Transfer weight forward onto LF		Three
8	RF to the side	Cha	Four
9	Close LF halfway to RF	Cha	and
10	RF a small step to the side	**Cha**	*One

When you have mastered these steps, practise rotating the figure slowly to the left.
This changes step 3 to *LF to the side and slightly back*.

Repeat as many times as you wish, then release your right hand for the New York.

Two

Three

Four

	THE NEW YORK		*One
Start position (feet not illustrated). Facing partner. Feet apart. Weight on RF.			
RH is released. Lead by extending your LH forward, turning partner to her left.			
1	Turn a quarter to the right. LF forward into LSP		Two
2	Transfer weight back onto RF, start turning to the left		Three
3	LF to the side, turning left to face partner (DH)	Cha	Four
4	Close RF halfway to LF (DH)	Cha	and
5	LF a small step to the side (releasing LH).	**Cha**	*One
----------------Lead by extending your RH forward turning partner to her right -----------------			
6	Turn a quarter to the left, RF forward into RSP		Two
7	Transfer weight back onto LF, start turning to the right		Three
8	RF to the side, turning right to face partner (DH)	Cha	Four
9	Close LF halfway to RF (DH)	Cha	and
10	RF a small step to the side (releasing RH)	**Cha**	*One

Repeat steps 1–5 then follow with the Spot Turn.

THE BASIC MOVEMENT

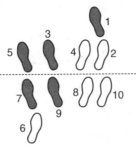

forward half

backward half

THE NEW YORK

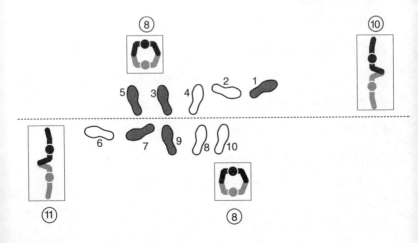

STEPS	**THE SPOT TURN**		BEATS

Start position (feet not illustrated). Feet apart. Weight on LF. LH is released.
With RH lead partner to turn to her right then release hold — *One

1	Turn a quarter to the left. RF forward		Two
2	Swivel both feet half a turn to the left, transfer weight forward to LF		Three
3	RF to the side, while still turning to the left	Cha	Four
4	Close LF halfway to RF, still turning	Cha	and
5	RF a small step to the side to face partner	**Cha**	*One

(Having completed a whole turn.)
The Spot Turn may also be danced stepping LF forward and — Two
turning right. Resume normal hold and follow with the Basic — Three
Movement or take double hold for the Hand to Hand. — Four

THE HAND TO HAND

and
Start position (feet not illustrated). Feet apart. Weight on RF. (DH.)
Lead by extending your RH forward, turning partner to her right, releasing LH. — *One

1	Turn a quarter to the left, LF back into RSP		Two
2	Transfer weight forward onto RF, start turning to the right		Three
3	LF to the side, turning right to face partner (DH)	Cha	Four
4	Close RF halfway to LF (DH)	Cha	and
5	LF a small step to the side (DH).	**Cha**	*One
	--Lead by extending your LH forward, turning partner to her left, releasing RH -------		
6	Turn a quarter to the right, RF back into LSP		Two
7	Transfer weight forward onto LF, start turning to the left		Three
8	RF to the side, turning left to face partner (DH)	Cha	Four
9	Close LF halfway to RF (DH)	Cha	and
10	RF a small step to the side (DH)	**Cha**	*One

Repeat as many times as you wish, then resume normal hold and follow
with the Basic Movement *or* repeat steps 1–5, and follow with the Spot Turn
before returning to the Basic Movement.

THE SPOT TURN

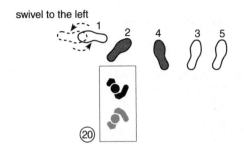

swivel to the left

THE HAND TO HAND

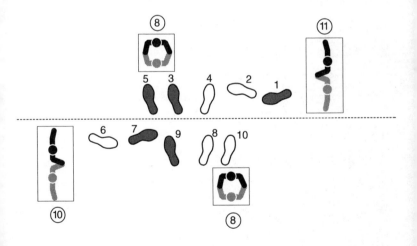

STEPS	**THE SHOULDER TO SHOULDER**		BEATS

Precede with the Basic Movement but turn slightly to the right on step 10.

Start position (feet not illustrated). Normal (or double) hold. ***One**

Weight on RF which is to the side and slightly forward.

1	LF forward outside your partner's left side		**Two**
2	Transfer weight back onto RF		**Three**
3	LF to the side turning slightly left	*Cha*	**Four**
4	Close RF halfway to LF, still turning	*Cha*	**and**
5	LF to side and slightly forward to right of partner,	***Cha***	***One**

----------------(completing a quarter turn to the left) ---

6	RF forward outside your partner's right side		**Two**
7	Transfer weight back onto LF		**Three**
8	RF to side turning slightly right	*Cha*	**Four**
9	Close LF halfway to RF, still turning	*Cha*	**and**
10	RF to side and slightly forward to left of partner,	***Cha***	***One**

(completing a quarter turn to the right)

Hold your partner firmly to keep her shoulders parallel with yours. Repeat as you **Two**
wish then, *either* turn to face your partner on step 10 for the Basic Movement,
or turn into PP, while repeating steps 1–5, to dance a Spot Turn to the left. **Three**

THE FAN

Four

The Fan: Start position (feet not illustrated) as in the Basic Movement. **and**

(Facing wall.) You dance the Basic Movement but lead differently. ***One**

(forward half)

1	LF forward		**Two**
2	Transfer weight back onto RF		**Three**
3	LF to the side	*Cha*	**Four**
4	Close RF halfway to LF	*Cha*	**and**
5	LF a small step to the side	***Cha***	***One**

----------------(backward half)---

6	RF back, leading partner towards you		**Two**
7	Transfer weight forward onto LF, turning partner towards your left side		**Three**
8	RF to the side. Release RH, partner steps back away from you	*Cha*	**Four**
9	Close LF halfway to RF	*Cha*	**and**
10	RF a small step to the side. Now in Fan Position	***Cha***	***One**

Follow with the Alemana or with the Hockey Stick.

THE SHOULDER TO SHOULDER

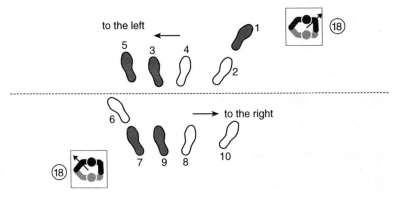

to the left

to the right

THE FAN

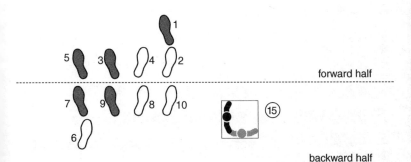

forward half

backward half

STEPS	**THE HOCKEY STICK**		BEATS

Start position (feet not illustrated). Fan position. Feet apart
Weight on RF. (Facing wall). Your partner's RH in your LH.   ***One**

1	LF forward		**Two**
2	Transfer weight back onto RF. Lead partner towards you with LH		**Three**
3	Close LF almost to RF. Lead partner towards you with LH waist high	*Cha*	**Four**
4	RF step on the spot while raising LH to lead partner in front of you	*Cha*	**and**
5	LF step on the spot. LH above partner	***Cha***	***One**

------------Your partner is in front and at a right angle to you ------------------------------------

6	Turn slightly right, cross RF behind LF, start turning partner to her left		**Two**
7	LF a small step forward, facing DW against LOD, still turning partner		**Three**
8	RF forward, lower LH, partner now facing you, moving backwards	*Cha*	**Four**
9	Close LF, with weight on ball, halfway to RF	*Cha*	**and**
10	RF forward – now in open facing position (facing DW against LOD)	***Cha***	***One**

Follow with the Basic Movement or with the Shoulder to Shoulder

	Two
	Three
	Four

THE ALEMANA

Start position (feet not illustrated). Fan position. Feet apart.   ***One**
Weight on RF. (Facing wall). Your partner's RH in your LH.

1	LF forward		**Two**
2	Transfer weight back onto RF. Lead partner towards you with LH		**Three**
3	Close LF to RF. Begin raising LH to lead partner towards you	*Cha*	**Four**
4	RF step on the spot, raising LH higher	*Cha*	**and**
5	LF step on the spot. LH above partner, start turning her to the right	***Cha***	***One**

--------------Your partner is in front and facing obliquely towards you--------------------------

6	RF back. Circle LH to turn partner to her right under raised hands		**Two**
7	Transfer weight forward onto LF, still turning partner		**Three**
8	Close RF to LF, still turning partner	*Cha*	**Four**
9	LF step on the spot, still turning partner	*Cha*	**and**
10	RF step on the spot. Resume normal hold	***Cha***	***One**

The **Woman's Underarm Turn to the Right.** Steps 6–10 may be danced
after steps 1–5 of the Basic Movement. Follow with the Basic Movement
or move RF to the side on step 10 to dance the Hand to Hand.

THE HOCKEY STICK

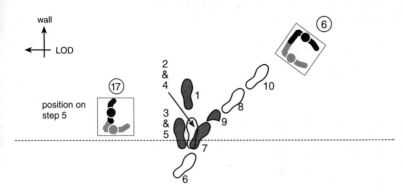

THE ALEMANA

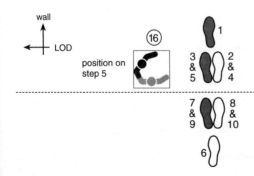

STEPS	**THE BASIC MOVEMENT**		BEATS
Start position (feet not illustrated). Feet apart. Normal hold.			
Weight on LF.			*One
(backward half)			
1	RF back		Two
2	Transfer weight forward onto LF		Three
3	RF to the side	Cha	Four
4	Close LF halfway to RF	Cha	and
5	RF a small step to the side	**Cha**	*One
--------------(forward half)--			
6	LF forward		Two
7	Transfer weight back onto RF		Three
8	LF to the side	Cha	Four
9	Close RF halfway to LF	Cha	and
10	LF a small step to the side	**Cha**	*One
When you have mastered these steps, practise rotating the figure slowly to the left.			
This changes step 8 to *LF to the side and slightly back.*			Two
Repeat as many times as necessary or your left hand will be released for			
the New York.			Three
			Four

	THE NEW YORK		
Start position (feet not illustrated). Facing partner. Feet apart. Weight on LF.			*One
LH is released. Your RH is extended forward leading you to turn.			
1	Turn a quarter to the left, RF forward into RSP		Two
2	Transfer weight back onto LF, start turning to the right		Three
3	RF to the side, turning right to face partner (DH)	Cha	Four
4	Close LF halfway to RF (DH)	Cha	and
5	RF a small step to the side (RH is released)	**Cha**	*One
----------------Your LH is extended forward leading you to turn ------------------------------------			
6	Turn a quarter to the right, LF forward into LSP		Two
7	Transfer weight back onto RF, start turning to the left		Three
8	LF to the side, turning left to face partner (DH)	Cha	Four
9	Close RF halfway to LF (DH)	Cha	and
10	LF a small step to the side (LH is released)	**Cha**	*One
Repeat steps 1–5 then follow with the Spot Turn.			

THE BASIC MOVEMENT

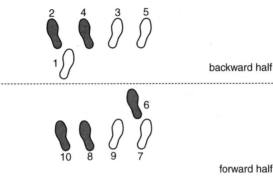

backward half

forward half

THE NEW YORK

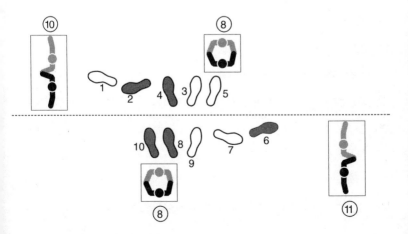

STEPS	**THE SPOT TURN**		BEATS

Start position (feet not illustrated). Feet apart. Weight on RF. RH is released.
Your LH will be drawn in front of you, to turn you, and then released.   ***One**

1	Turn a quarter to the right. LF forward		**Two**

2	Swivel both feet half a turn right, transfer weight forward onto RF		**Three**

3	LF to the side, while still turning to the right	*Cha*	**Four**
4	Close RF halfway to LF, still turning	*Cha*	and
5	LF a small step to the side to face partner	***Cha***	***One**

(Having completed a whole turn.)

This may also be danced stepping off RF forward and turning left.   **Two**

Resume normal hold and follow with the Basic Movement or take
double hold for the Hand to Hand.   **Three**

THE HAND TO HAND   **Four**

Start position (feet not illustrated). Feet apart. Weight on LF. (DH.)   and
Your RH is released while your LH is extended forward to lead you to turn.   ***One**

1	Turn a quarter to the right, RF back into LSP		**Two**

2	Transfer weight forward onto LF, start turning to the left		**Three**

3	RF to the side, turning left to face partner (DH)	*Cha*	**Four**
4	Close LF halfway to RF (DH)	*Cha*	and
5	RF a small step to the side (DH)	***Cha***	***One**

-------------Your LH is released while your RH is extended forward -----------------------

6	Turn a quarter to the left, LF back into RSP		**Two**

7	Transfer weight forward onto RF, start turning to the right		**Three**

8	LF to the side, turning right to face partner (DH)	*Cha*	**Four**
9	Close RF halfway to LF (DH)	*Cha*	and
10	LF a small step to the side (DH)	***Cha***	***One**

Repeat as many times as necessary, then resume normal hold and follow with the
Basic Movement *or* repeat steps 1–5, and follow with the Spot Turn before returning
to the Basic Movement.

THE SPOT TURN

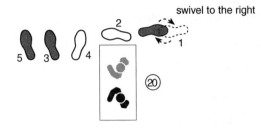

swivel to the right

THE HAND TO HAND

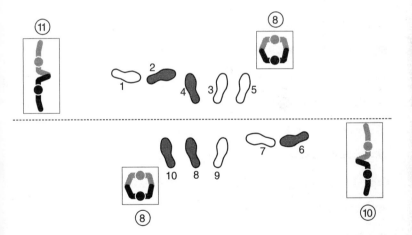

STEPS	**THE SHOULDER TO SHOULDER**		BEATS
	Start position (feet not illustrated).		
	Normal (or double) hold. Weight on LF which is to the side and		*One
	slightly back having turned slightly to the right on the previous step.		
1	RF back. Your partner is outside on your left		Two
2	Transfer weight forward onto LF		Three
3	RF to the side turning slightly left	Cha	Four
4	Close LF halfway to RF, still turning	Cha	and
5	RF to the side and slightly back. Your partner is a little to your right	**Cha**	*One

----------------Thus completing a quarter turn to the left-----------------------------------

6	LF back, your partner is outside on your right		Two
7	Transfer weight forward onto RF		Three
8	LF to the side turning slightly right	Cha	Four
9	Close RF halfway to LF, still turning	Cha	and
10	LF to side and slightly back. Your partner is a little to your left	**Cha**	*One
	Thus completing a quarter turn to the right.		

Repeat as many times as you wish then, *either* turn to face your partner
on step 10 to follow with the Basic Movement, *or* turn into PP,

		Two
while repeating steps 1–5, and follow with a Spot Turn to the right.		Three

	THE FAN		Four
			and
	Start position (feet not illustrated). Normal hold. Feet apart, weight on LF.		*One
	(Facing centre.)		
1	RF back		Two
2	Transfer weight forward onto LF		Three
3	RF to the side	Cha	Four
4	Close LF halfway to RF	Cha	and
5	RF a small step to the side	**Cha**	*One
6	LF forward then turn a quarter to the left		Two
7	RF back and slightly to the side, now facing your partner's left side		Three
8	LF back on *ball of foot*, moving away from partner. LH is released	Cha	Four
9	Close RF halfway to LF	Cha	and
10	LF back, now in Fan Position. (Facing against LOD)	**Cha**	*One

Follow with the Alemana or with the Hockey Stick.

THE SHOULDER TO SHOULDER

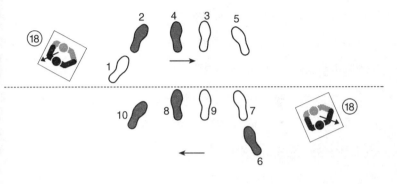

THE FAN

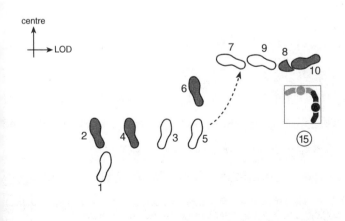

STEPS	**THE HOCKEY STICK**		BEATS

Start position (left foot illustrated). Fan position. LF back.
Weight on LF. (Facing against LOD.) RH in partner's LH. — ***One**

1	Close RF to LF		**Two**
2	LF forward as you are led towards your partner		**Three**
3	RF forward as your RH is gradually raised	*Cha*	**Four**
4	Close LF *on ball* halfway to RF. RH is still being raised	*Cha*	and
5	RF forward a small step (your right side is in front of partner)	***Cha***	***One**
6	Turning left, LF forward (facing DW against LOD)		**Two**
7	Extend RF forward, swivel a half turn left. Transfer weight to RF		**Three**
8	LF back on *ball of foot* as RH is lowered. (Now facing partner)	*Cha*	**Four**
9	Close RF halfway to LF	*Cha*	and
10	LF back, now in open facing position	***Cha***	***One**

Follow with the Basic Movement or with the Shoulder to Shoulder.

Two

Three

	THE ALEMANA		**Four**

Start position (left foot illustrated). Fan position. LF back. Weight on LF.
(Facing against LOD.) RH in partner's LH. — ***One**

1	Close RF to LF		**Two**
2	LF forward moving towards your partner		**Three**
3	RF forward as your RH is raised	*Cha*	**Four**
4	Close LF on *ball of foot* halfway to RF as your RH is raised higher	*Cha*	and
5	RF a small forward step, curving right in front of your partner	***Cha***	***One**
6	Continue turning right under raised hands, LF forward (facing LOD)		**Two**
7	Still turning, RF forward (facing DW against LOD)		**Three**
8	LF a small step forward turning right under raised hands	*Cha*	**Four**
9	RF a *semi closing* step on ball of foot	*Cha*	and
10	LF a small step forward to face partner having	***Cha***	***One**

completed one and a quarter turns. Resume normal hold.

The **Woman's Underarm Turn to the Right.** Steps 6–10 may be danced
after steps 1–5 of the Basic Movement (completing one turn). Follow with
the Basic Movement *or* dance the Hand to Hand.

THE HOCKEY STICK   **THE ALEMANA**

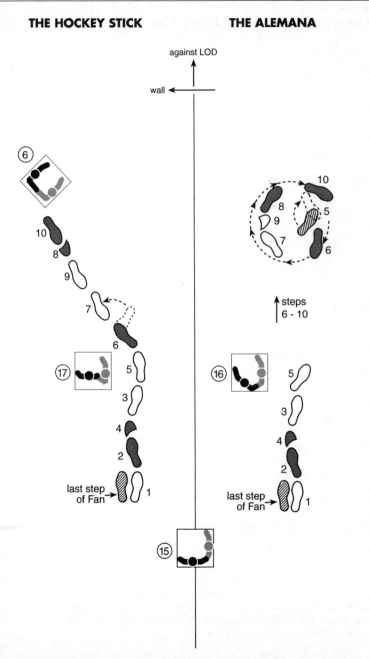

against LOD

wall ←

⑥

10
8
9

7

6

⑰   5

3

4

2

last step of Fan → 1

steps 6 - 10

10
8
9
7
5
6

⑯   5

3

4

2

last step of Fan → 1

⑮

Perfecting your Cha-cha-cha technique

Starting

Because the first step of each figure is made on a bar's second beat, many beginners find starting difficult. Some dancers, having transferred weight on the bar's heavy first beat, step off on beat two as we have indicated. Others count *one*, *two*, *three*, dance a sideways chassé on beats four and one and then, on beat two, make their first forward or backward linking step.

Footwork and hip action

Your knee is flexed (slightly bent) at the beginning of each step when the ball of your foot is pressed *firmly* into the floor. Your weight is then transferred quickly to this foot as the knee straightens and the heel lowers while your other knee flexes and your other heel lifts. This *ball flat* foot/ankle/knee movement, which makes your hips swing towards the foot that is taking your weight, produces the cha-cha-cha *hip action* which characterizes every step of the dance, although it is less noticeable on the quicker steps. To avoid loss of balance, lowering the heel is delayed slightly when you step back.

Your upper body is always held upright over your front foot when taking a forward or backward step. Correct poise and balance must be coupled with strong foot, ankle and leg action to achieve the crisp rhythmic feeling that is the hallmark of the Cha-cha-cha.

Free arms

During *one-hand holds*, which occur in many figures, your free arm should be extended sideways in a gentle curve so that your hand is held, palm down, just above your waist level. The poised position of the upper body and the arm's flowing movements contrast with the abrupt action of the legs and hips.

Partner's roles

In many figures the woman turns under her partner's arm or moves away and then returns to him. She makes the elaborate steps; he has the task of choreographing the dance, leading her firmly but gently nto each figure and avoiding collisions. The man should lead: the woman should follow.

The dance's mood

Couples can best express the brisk and lively mood of the Cha-cha-cha by responding to its music with firm steps and strong leg actions, by rotating the Basic Movement and by changing dance positions with smooth arm movements as they move from one figure to the next.

Alternative choreographies

a Basic Movement.
  Lady's Underarm Turn
      to the Right.
  Hand to Hand.
  Spot Turn to the left
      (woman's right).

b Basic Movement.
  New York.
  Spot Turn to the left
      (woman's right).
  Hand to Hand.
  Spot Turn to the left
      (woman's right).

c Basic Movement.
  Shoulder to Shoulder
      three times.
  Woman's Underarm Turn to
      the Right.

d Basic Movement.
  Fan.
  Hockey Stick.
  Alemana from open
      facing position.
  (Woman steps back
      on step 1).

e Basic Movement.
  Fan, Hockey Stick
      overturned to LSP
      (woman RSP).
  New York twice.
  Spot Turn to the right
      (woman's left).
  Spot Turn to the left
      (woman's right).

f Basic Movement.
  Fan.
  Alemana.
  Shoulder to Shoulder.
  Spot Turn to the left
      (woman's right).

3 | RUMBA

The Rumba, often called the dance of love, has music in 4/4 time (four beats to each bar) and a fairly slow tempo (about 27 bars per minute). Three steps are danced during each bar – the third being taken over two beats – to give a quick-quick-slow rhythm. Many of its figures have counterparts in the Cha-cha-cha but, being slower, the Rumba's step pattern is easier for beginners. It has a softer beat and a subtler, more sensuous rhythm to which dancers' hip and leg movements make an appropriate response.

In the eighteenth and nineteenth centuries a large family of dances including the *Son*, the *Son Montuno*, the *Danzon* and the *Guajira* took root in Cuba and other Spanish Caribbean possessions. Each had a Rumba rhythm – although their tempos varied. Some are still danced in parts of Latin America.

The inspiration for these 'Rumbas' almost certainly come from three continents. Native Indians had brought the *Cueca*, Chile's national folk dance – which mimicked the courting walk of a cock – from South America's Pacific coast. The colonists had brought their traditional *Bolero* from Spain. Then, between 1680 and 1786, black slaves introduced a primitive ritual dance from Africa.

American jazz came to Cuba in the 1920s and an Americanized Rumba, the *Square Rumba*, became popular in the US and soon after crossed the Atlantic. Ten years later two notable teachers – 'Monsieur' Pierre, a Basque, and his partner Doris Lavelle introduced the *Cuban Rumba* to Londoners. When the Americans sailed for home after the war it was this Cuban version that gained popularity and, in 1955, became the officially recognized dance in Britain.

Holds

Start facing your partner, about six inches (150 mm) away, in an upright position with your head erect. The man's right hand should be placed on the woman's left shoulder blade while her left arm is laid on his right, with her hand resting on his shoulder. Joined hands should be held lightly and raised to the man's eye level providing he is not a lot taller than his partner. This is called *normal hold* but, in Latin dances, your position in relation to your partner changes frequently. Some figures are danced with both hands held (*double hold*) some with one hand held (*one hand hold*) and some without hold.

The Basic Movement on pages 34 (man) and 42 (woman) has a forward and a backward half. Practise it until you can dance it with ease. It is the foundation on which all other figures rest.

Footwork

Footwork to be ball flat.

Figure 3.1   Normal hold position

STEPS	**THE BASIC MOVEMENT**	BEATS

Start position (feet not illustrated). Normal hold. Feet apart, weight on RF.

*One

(forward half)

1 Q LF forward — Two

2 Q Transfer weight back onto RF — Three

3 ▌ LF to the side — Four

3 ▐S▌ Hold position — *One

----------------(backward half)--

4 Q RF back — Two

5 Q Transfer weight forward onto LF — Three

6 ▌ RF to the side — Four

6 ▐S▌ Hold position — *One

When you have mastered these steps, practise rotating the figure gently to the left.
This changes step 3 to *LF to the side and slightly back*. — Two
Repeat as you wish or release your RH and extend your LH forward
to lead into the New York (see the Cha-cha-cha). — Three

Four

THE SIDE STEP

Start position (feet illustrated). Normal hold. Weight on RF, having, on the last — *One
step of the Basic Movement, stepped RF *forward* and closed LF to it without weight.

1 Q LF to the side — Two

2 Q Close RF to LF — Three

3 ▌ LF to the side — Four

3 ▐S▌ Hold position — *One

4 Q Close RF to LF — Two

5 Q LF to the side — Three

6 ▌ Close RF to LF — Four

6 ▐S▌ Hold position — *One

Either follow with the Basic Movement or with a LF Cucaracha.

THE BASIC MOVEMENT

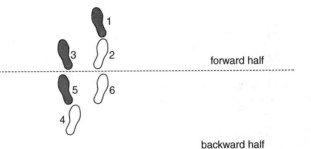

forward half

backward half

THE SIDE STEP

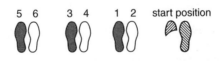

STEPS   **THE CUCARACHA (PRESSURE STEP)**   BEATS

Start position (feet not illustrated). Normal hold.
Feet together, weight on RF (having danced the Side Step).   ***One**

1 Q LF to side, keeping RF flat while circling hips anti-clockwise	**Two**
2 Q Transfer weight sideways to RF	**Three**
3 Close LF to RF	**Four**
3 S Hold position	***One**

The Cucaracha may also be danced starting with the RF.
Follow with *either* an RF Cucaracha *or* with the Woman's Underarm Turn   **Two**
to the Right.

Three

THE SHOULDER TO SHOULDER   **Four**

Start position (feet not illustrated). Normal hold. Weight on RF
which is to the side and slightly forward having turned slightly to right on   ***One**
previous step in preparation for:

1 Q LF forward outside your partner's left side	**Two**
2 Q Transfer weight back to RF	**Three**
3 Turn a quarter to the left, LF to side and slightly forward	**Four**
3 S Hold position. (You are to the right of your partner)	***One**
4 Q RF forward outside your partner's right side	**Two**
5 Q Transfer weight back to LF	**Three**
6 Turn a quarter to the right, RF to side and slightly forward	**Four**
6 S Hold position. (You are to the left of your partner)	***One**

Hold your partner firmly to keep her shoulders parallel with yours.
Repeat as you wish then *either* turn to face your partner on step 6
to follow with the Basic Movement *or* turn into PP,
while repeating steps 1–3, and follow with the Spot Turn to the
left (as in the Cha-cha-cha).

THE CUCARACHA (PRESSURE STEP)

LF CUCARACHA

1   3 2
(also start
position)

RF CUCARACHA

2 3   1
(also start
position)

THE SHOULDER TO SHOULDER

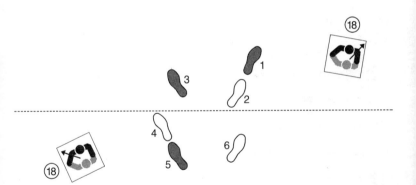

STEPS	**THE HAND TO HAND**	BEATS

Start position (feet not illustrated). Feet apart, weight on RF (DH).
Lead by extending your RH forward, turning partner to her right,   ***One**
releasing LH.

1 Q Turn a quarter to the left, LF back into RSP	**Two**

2 Q Transfer weight forward onto RF, start turning to the right	**Three**

3 LF to the side turning right to face partner (DH)	**Four**

3 S Hold position	***One**

------- Lead by extending your LH forward, turning partner to her left, releasing RH----------

4 Q Turn a quarter to the right, RF back into LSP	**Two**

5 Q Transfer weight forward onto LF, start turning to the left	**Three**

6 RF to the side, turning left to face partner (DH)	**Four**

6 S Hold position	***One**

Repeat as you wish, then *either* resume normal hold and follow with the
Basic Movement *or* repeat steps 1–3 and follow with the Spot Turn to the left,   **Two**
as in the Cha-cha-cha, before returning to the Basic Movement.

    Three

THE FAN

Start position (feet not illustrated). Normal hold, feet apart, weight on RF.   **Four**
(Facing wall.) (The steps are the same as in the Basic Movement but
you lead your partner differently during steps 4–6.)   ***One**
    (forward half)

1 Q LF forward	**Two**

2 Q Transfer weight back onto RF	**Three**

3 LF to the side	**Four**

3 S Hold position	***One**

--------(backward half)--

4 Q RF back, leading partner towards you	**Two**

5 Q Transfer weight onto LF. Turn partner towards your left side.	**Three**
(Release RH)	

6 RF to the side, leading partner to step backwards	**Four**

6 S Hold her in Fan position	***One**

Follow with the Alemana or with the Hockey Stick.

THE HAND TO HAND

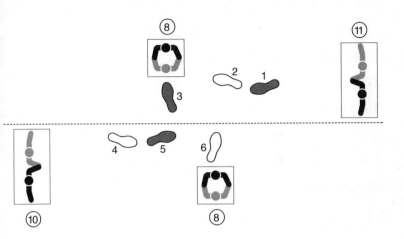

THE FAN

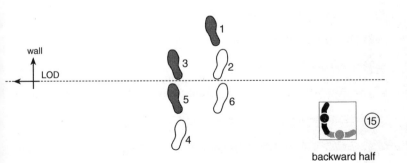

backward half

STEPS	**THE HOCKEY STICK**	BEATS

Start position (feet not illustrated). Fan position. Feet apart, weight on RF. (Facing wall.) Hold your partner's RH in your LH.   ***One**

1 Q LF forward   **Two**

2 Q Transfer weight back onto RF. Lead partner towards you   **Three**

3 Close LF to RF. LH raised above partner   **Four**

3 S Hold position   ***One**

--------Your partner is in front and at a right angle to you ---

4 Q Turn slightly right, cross RF behind LF   **Two**

5 Q LF a small step forward, still turning partner (Facing DW against LOD)   **Three**

6 RF forward while lowering LH, to finish in Open Facing Position   **Four**

6 S Hold position (facing DW against LOD)   ***One**

Follow with the Basic Movement or with the Shoulder to Shoulder.

    Two

    Three

    Four

THE ALEMANA

Start position (feet not illustrated). Fan position. Feet apart, weight on RF. (Facing wall.) Hold your partner's RH in your LH.   ***One**

1 Q LF forward   **Two**

2 Q Transfer weight back onto RF. Raise LH to draw partner close   **Three**

3 Close LF to RF. Start turning partner to her right   **Four**

3 S Hold position   ***One**

--------Your partner is in front and facing obliquely towards you -----------------------------------

4 Q RF back. Circle LH to turn partner to her right under raised hands   **Two**

5 Q Transfer weight forward onto LF, still turning partner   **Three**

6 Close RF to LF. Resume normal hold   **Four**

6 S Hold position   ***One**

The Woman's Underarm Turn to the Right. As a simpler alternative, steps 4–6 may be danced after steps 1–3 of the Basic Movement. Follow with *either* the Basic Movement *or* an LF Cucaracha *or*, on 6, step RF to the side and take double hold to follow with the Hand to Hand.

THE HOCKEY STICK

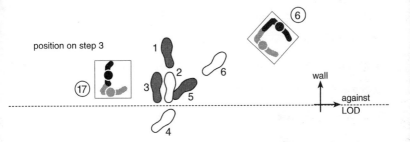

position on step 3

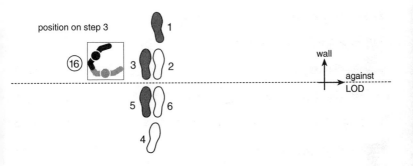

THE ALEMANA

position on step 3

STEPS	**THE BASIC MOVEMENT**	BEATS

Start position (feet not illustrated). Normal hold. Feet apart, weight on LF.

*One

(backward half)

1 Q RF back — Two

2 Q Transfer weight forward onto LF — Three

3 RF to the side — Four

3 S Hold position — *One

----------------(forward half)---

4 Q LF forward — Two

5 Q Transfer weight back onto RF — Three

6 LF to the side — Four

6 S Hold position — *One

When you have mastered these steps, practise rotating them slowly to the left.
This changes step 6 to *LF to the side and slightly back.* Repeat as necessary. — Two
If your LH is released and your RH is extended forward, your partner
is leading you into the New York (as Cha-cha-cha). — Three

THE SIDE STEP — Four

Start position (feet illustrated). Normal hold. Weight on LF, having, on the last
step of the Basic Movement, stepped *back* with the LF and closed the RF to it — *One
without weight.

1 Q RF to the side — Two

2 Q Close LF to RF — Three

3 RF to the side — Four

3 S Hold position — *One

4 Q Close LF to RF — Two

5 Q RF to the side — Three

6 Close LF to RF — Four

6 S Hold position — *One

Either follow with the Basic Movement or with a RF Cucaracha.

THE BASIC MOVEMENT

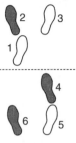

backward half

forward half

THE SIDE STEP

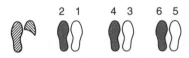

STEPS	**THE CUCARACHA (PRESSURE STEP)**	BEATS

Start position (feet not illustrated). Normal hold.
Feet together, weight on LF (having danced the Side Step)   ***One**

1 Q RF to side with pressure, keeping LF flat. Circle hips clockwise	**Two**

2 Q Transfer weight sideways to LF	**Three**

3 Close RF to LF	**Four**

3 S Hold position	***One**

The Cucaracha may also be danced starting with the LF.
Follow with *either* a LF Cucaracha *or* with the Woman's Underarm Turn to   **Two**
the Right.

   Three

THE SHOULDER TO SHOULDER

Precede with the Basic Movement but turn slightly to your right on step 6.   **Four**
Your partner will be slightly to the left of you. Start position (feet not illustrated).
Normal hold. Weight on LF which is to the side and slightly back.   ***One**

1 Q RF back (your partner is outside on your left)	**Two**

2 Q Transfer weight forward onto LF	**Three**

3 Turn a quarter to the left, RF to side and slightly back	**Four**

3 S Hold position. (Your partner is slightly to your right)	***One**

4 Q LF back (your partner is outside on your right)	**Two**

5 Q Transfer weight forward onto RF	**Three**

6 Turn a quarter to the right. LF to the side and slightly back	**Four**

6 S Hold position. (Your partner is slightly to your left)	***One**

Keep parallel to your partner as you turn from left to right.
Repeat as you wish then *either* turn to face your partner on step 6 to follow
with the Basic Movement *or* turn into PP, while repeating steps 1–3,
and follow with the Spot Turn to the right (as in the Cha-cha-cha).

THE CUCARACHA (PRESSURE STEP)

LF CUCARACHA   **RF CUCARACHA**

1   3 2
(also start
position)

2 3   1
(also start
position)

THE SHOULDER TO SHOULDER

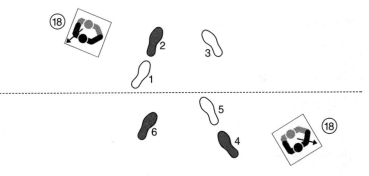

STEPS	**THE HAND TO HAND**	BEATS

Start position (feet not illustrated). Feet apart, weight on LF (DH).
Your RH is released while your LH is extended forward, to lead you to turn. ***One**

1 Q Turn a quarter to the right, RF back into LSP	**Two**

2 Q Transfer weight forward onto LF, start turning to the left	**Three**

3 ● RF to the side turning left to face partner (DH)	**Four**

3 S Hold position	***One**

------- Your LH is released while your RH is extended forward, to lead you to turn-----------

4 Q Turn a quarter to the left, LF back into RSP	**Two**

5 Q Transfer weight forward onto RF, start turning to the right	**Three**

6 ● LF to the side, turning right to face partner (DH)	**Four**

6 S Hold position	***One**

Repeat as many times as necessary, then *either* resume normal hold and follow
with the Basic Movement *or* repeat steps 1–3 and follow with the Spot Turn
to the right, as in the Cha-cha-cha, before returning to the Basic Movement. **Two**

Three

Four

THE FAN

Start position (feet not illustrated). Normal hold, feet apart, weight on LF. ***One**
(Facing centre.)

1 Q RF back	**Two**

2 Q Transfer weight forward onto LF	**Three**

3 ● RF to the side	**Four**

3 S Hold position	***One**

4 Q LF forward, then turn a quarter to your left	**Two**

5 Q RF back and slightly to the side (now facing partner's left side)	**Three**
Release LH	

6 ● LF back, now in Fan position. (Facing against LOD)	**Four**

6 S Hold position	***One**

Follow with *either* the Alemana *or* the Hockey Stick.

THE HAND TO HAND

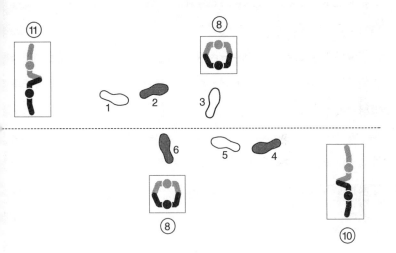

THE FAN

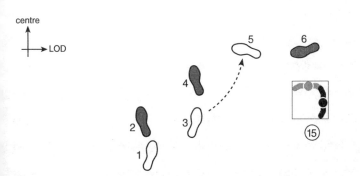

STEPS	**THE HOCKEY STICK**	BEATS
Start position (left foot illustrated). Fan position. LF back, weight on LF. (Facing against LOD). RH in partner's LH.		*One
1 Q Close RF to LF		Two
2 Q LF forward, moving towards your partner (RH kept low)		Three
3 ▌ RF forward in front of partner at a right angle to him (RH raised)		Four
3 ▌S Hold position		*One
4 Q LF forward, curving left (facing DW against LOD)		Two
5 Q Extend RF forward, swivel half turn left. Weight now on RF. (Facing DC)		Three
6 ▌ Now in open facing position. LF back		Four
6 ▌S Hold position		*One

Follow with the Basic Movement or with the Shoulder to Shoulder.

		Two
		Three
		Four

	THE ALEMANA	
Start position (left foot illustrated). Fan position. LF back, weight on LF. (Facing against LOD). RH in partner's LH.		*One
1 Q Close RF to LF		Two
2 Q LF forward, moving towards partner and raising RH		Three
3 ▌ RF forward, curving to the right in front of your partner		Four
3 ▌S Hold position		*One
4 Q Continue turning right under raised hands. LF forward (facing LOD)		Two
5 Q Still turning, RF forward (facing DW against LOD)		Three
6 ▌ Still turning to face partner. LF a small step forward		Four
6 ▌S Hold position. Resume normal hold.		*One

The Woman's Underarm Turn to the Right. As a simpler alternative, steps 4–6 may be danced after steps 1–3 of the Basic Movement. Follow with *either* the Basic Movement *or* an RF Cucaracha *or*, if your partner takes double hold, with the Hand to Hand.

THE HOCKEY STICK

THE ALEMANA

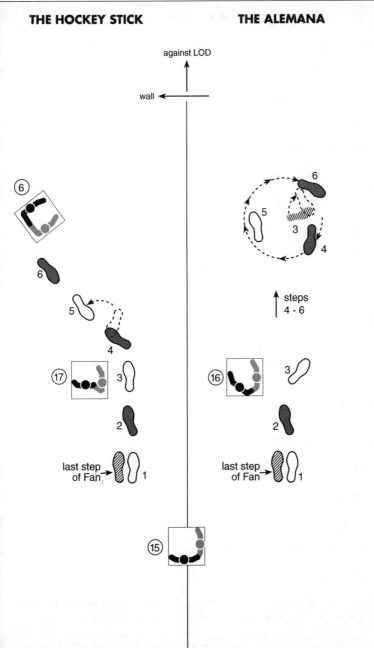

against LOD

wall

steps
4 - 6

last step
of Fan

last step
of Fan

Perfecting your Rumba technique

Starting

Because the first step of each figure is taken on a bar's second beat (rather than on the more emphatic first beat) you will find it helpful to swing your hips and transfer your weight to the side (men to the right, women to the left) on beat one before stepping off on beat two.

Footwork and hip action

This is similar to the Cha-cha-cha, but less hurried and therefore smoother. Your knee is flexed (slightly bent) at the beginning of each step when the ball of your foot is pressed *firmly* into the floor. Your weight is then transferred to this foot as the knee straightens and the heel lowers while your other knee flexes and your other heel lifts. This *ball flat* ankle/knee movement makes your hips sway over the foot that has taken your weight. When you step back, delay transferring weight for an instant. Holding it momentarily over your forward foot helps you to keep your balance. During two-beat steps (every third step) the weight is transferred on beat four and held during beat one. Both legs are straight while the hips complete their sway.

To maintain control, preserve your balance and ensure smooth movements, keep your toes in contact with the floor while taking each step.

Progressive walks

Groups of three or six walking steps, which may be danced forwards or backwards – in a straight line or in a curve – are all called Progressive Walks. They are danced in *normal hold* or *one hand hold*.

The forward walks, which start with the left foot, follow the backward half of the Basic Movement, the last step of which goes forward (instead of to the side). The backward walks follow the forward half of the Basic Movement, the last step of which goes back.

Free arms

During *one hand holds*, your free arm should be extended sideways in a gentle curve so that your hand is held palm down, just above your waist level. The figure's pattern will look much more attractive if your arm's continuous, unaffected movement is smoothly co-ordinated with your steps.

Partner's roles

In many figures the woman turns under her partner's arm or moves away and then returns to him. She makes the elaborate steps. He is her choreographer who leads her firmly yet gently into each figure and protects her from collisions. When she turns under raised arms, he must ensure that their joined hands are above her head so that her balance is not disturbed. He must lead. She must follow.

The dance's mood

The Rumba is a stage on which a woman can give a sensuous display of her femininity and poise before a partner who is masterful but indolent.

Alternative choreographies

Most of the following figures have counterparts in the Cha-cha-cha.

a Basic Movement.
   Shoulder to Shoulder three
      times.
   Woman's Underarm Turn
      to the Right.

b Basic Movement.
   The Side Step.
   3 Cucarachas.
   Woman's Underarm Turn
      to the Right.
   Hand to Hand.
   Spot Turn to the left
      (woman's right).

c Basic Movement.
   The Fan.
   The Hockey Stick.
   1–3 of Basic Movement.
      (One Hand Hold.)
   6 Back Walks (woman
      forward). (One Hand
      Hold.)
   Woman's Underarm Turn to
      the Right.

d Basic Movement.
   The Fan.
   The Alemana.
   Hand to Hand.
   Spot Turn to the left
      (woman's right).

4 | MAMBO

The Mambo is another of the Cha-cha-cha/Rumba family of dances. It has a fast, exciting, lively rhythm, like a quick Rumba, to which a variety of percussion instruments contribute. The music, in 4/4 time (four beats to each bar) has a quick tempo (40–56 bars per minute).

The cosmopolitan island of Cuba, with its unique Caribbean mix of South American Indian, African and Spanish races, was the Mambo's cradle. In Cuba, during the nineteenth and twentieth centuries, the Mambo survived opposition from the establishment and onslaughts from the church and became popular. And from Cuba, with the ending of the Second World War, the Mambo was spread, by films, recordings and tourists, throughout the Americas, Europe and English-speaking Asia.

As in the Rumba, three steps are taken during each four-beat bar of music. Because the third step is held during the fourth beat, the result is a *quick-quick-slow* rhythm. Many figures rotate about a spot, like the basic movements in the Cha-cha-cha and Rumba. Because of the quick tempo, steps are kept small and the result is a notably staccato leg action with less emphasis on hip action than in the Rumba and Cha-cha-cha. There are, however, many welcome rock actions on the spot – some made with the feet apart, others with the feet together – which link figures and provide breathing pauses.

Normal hold

This position is similar to the normal hold in the Rumba except that it is closer and a little more upright. Also, to provide control while stepping quickly, the arms and upper body are kept braced.

The Closed Basic has a forward and a backward half. Practise it until you can dance it with ease then add extra figures, one at a time, before dancing the Closed Basic again.

Footwork

Footwork to be ball flat unless instructed otherwise.

Figure 4.1   Normal hold position

STEPS	**THE CLOSED BASIC**	BEATS

Start position (feet not illustrated). Normal hold.
Feet together, weight on RF. | | *One
      (forward half)

1 Q LF forward with toes turned out	**Two**

2 Q Transfer weight back onto RF	**Three**

3 Close LF to RF	**Four**

3 S Hold position	***One**

----------------(backward half)----------------

4 Q RF back on ball of foot	**Two**

5 Q Transfer weight forward onto LF	**Three**

6 Close RF to LF	**Four**

6 S Hold position	***One**

When you have mastered these steps, practise rotating the figure to the left.
Taking a side step on 3 and on 6 is another variant which, incidentally, makes rotating the figure easier. | **Two**

Three

	THE PROGRESSIVE BACK	**Four**

Start position (feet not illustrated). Normal hold.
Feet together, weight on RF. | | *One
      (forward half)

1 Q LF forward with toes turned out	**Two**

2 Q Transfer weight back onto RF	**Three**

3 LF back	**Four**

3 S Hold position	***One**

----------------(backward half)----------------

4 Q RF back on ball of foot	**Two**

5 Q Transfer weight forward onto LF	**Three**

6 RF forward	**Four**

6 S Hold position	***One**

This figure is not rotated. Repeat as many times as you wish.

THE CLOSED BASIC

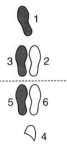

forward half

backward half

THE PROGRESSIVE BASIC

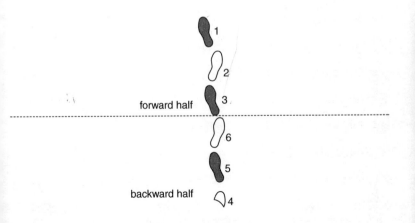

STEPS **SECOND POSITION BREAKS (CUCARACHAS)**	BEATS
Start position (feet illustrated). Normal hold.	
Feet together, weight on RF.	*One

1 Q LF to the side with *part weight*	Two

2 Q Transfer all weight sideways onto RF	Three

3 Close LF to RF	Four
S	
3 Hold position	*One

----

4 Q RF to the side with *part weight*	Two

5 Q Transfer all weight sideways onto LF	Three

6 Close RF to LF	Four
S	
6 Hold position	*One

Repeat as many times as you wish. Follow with the Closed,
The Progressive, or the Turning Basic.

Two

Three

CROSS-OVER BREAKS (THE NEW YORK)

Precede with the Closed Basic but step to the side on step 6.

Four

Start position (feet not illustrated). Facing partner, feet apart, weight on RF,
RH is released.

*One

Lead by extending your LH forward, turning partner to her left.

1 Q Turn a quarter to the right. LF forward into LSP	Two

2 Q Transfer weight back onto RF, start turning to the left	Three

3 LF to the side, turning left to face partner (DH)	Four
S	
3 Hold position	*One

-------Lead by extending RH forward, turning partner to her right, releasing LH-------------

4 Q Turn a quarter to the left. RF forward into RSP	Two

5 Q Transfer weight back onto LF, start turning to the right	Three

6 RF to the side, turning right to face partner (DH)	Four
S	
6 Hold position	*One

Repeat as many times as you wish, then repeat steps 1 to 3
before following with the Spot Turn to the left (as in the
Cha-cha-cha and the Rumba).

SECOND POSITION BREAKS (CUCARACHAS)

1   3 2

also start
position

5 6   4

also start
position

CROSS-OVER BREAKS (THE NEW YORK)

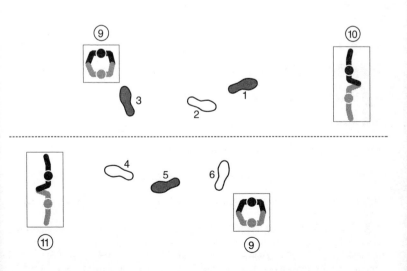

STEPS	**THE BACK BREAK**	BEATS
Start position (feet not illustrated). Normal or double hold. Feet together, weight on RF. (Steps are as the Closed Basic but you lead differently during 4–6.) (forward half)		*One
1 Q LF forward with toes turned out		Two
2 Q Transfer weight back onto RF		Three
3 LF a small step to the side of RF		Four
3 Hold position		*One

------------------(backward half) --

4 Q RF back onto ball of foot. Extend arms so your partner steps back		Two
5 Q Transfer weight forward onto LF. Draw your partner towards you		Three
6 Close RF to LF. (Return to start position)		Four
6 Hold position		*One

Repeat as many times as you wish. This figure is not rotated.
Follow with the Closed Basic, the Second Position Break or the Double Back Break.

	Two
	Three
	Four

THE DOUBLE BACK BREAK

Start position (feet not illustrated). Normal or double hold. Feet together, weight on RF.		*One
1 Q LF back onto ball of foot. Extend arms so your partner steps back		Two
2 Q Transfer weight forward onto RF. Draw your partner towards you		Three
3 Close RF to LF. (Return to start position)		Four
3 Hold position		*One

----

4 Q RF back onto ball of foot. Extend arms so your partner steps back		Two
5 Q Transfer weight forward onto LF. Draw your partner towards you		Three
6 Close RF to LF. (Return to start position)		Four
6 Hold position		*One

As an alternative, you may raise your left arm after step 3, so that your partner turns to her right under your joined hands during steps 4, 5 and 6, before you resume normal hold. Follow with the Closed, the Progressive, or the Turning Basic or with the Second Position Break.

THE BACK BREAK

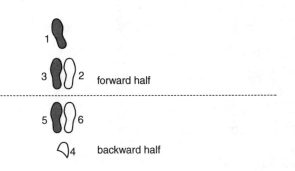

THE DOUBLE BACK BREAK

| STEPS | **THE TURNING BASIC** | BEATS |

Start position (feet not illustrated). Facing wall in normal hold.
Feet together, weight on RF.   *One

1 Q LF forward with toes turned out   Two

2 Q Transfer weight back onto RF. Start turning to the left   Three

3 Turn a quarter to the left to face LOD. LF to the side, into PP   Four
S
3 Hold position   *One

4 Q Turning left to face centre, RF back, drawing partner towards you   Two

5 Q Transfer weight forward onto LF   Three

6 RF forward. (Return to start position.) (Facing centre)   Four
S
6 Hold position   *One

To make the turn comfortable, take small steps and keep your hold close. As an easier
alternative, on step 4, the quarter turn may be omitted so that you remain facing   Two
the LOD. Repeat as many times as you wish before following with Closed Basic.

                                                                    Three

SPOT TURNS TO RIGHT AND LEFT   Four

Start position (feet not illustrated). Facing wall, feet apart, weight on RF
(having stepped to the side on the last step of the previous figure). RH is   *One
released. With LH, lead partner to turn to her left then release hold.

1 Q Turn a quarter to the right. LF forward. (Facing against LOD)   Two

2 Q Turn a half turn to the right. Transfer weight forward onto RF.   Three
(Facing LOD)
3 LF to side while completing a whole turn to face partner   Four
S
3 Hold position   *One

4 Q Turn a quarter to the left. RF forward. (Facing LOD)   Two

5 Q Turn a half turn to the left. Transfer weight forward onto LF.   Three
(Facing against LOD)
6 RF to side while completing a whole turn to face partner   Four
S
6 Resume normal hold then hold position   *One

The body movement initiates the turn. Keep the body braced and the steps small.
Follow with the Closed, the Progressive, or the Turning Basic.

THE TURNING BASIC

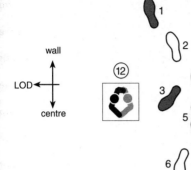

SPOT TURNS TO RIGHT AND LEFT

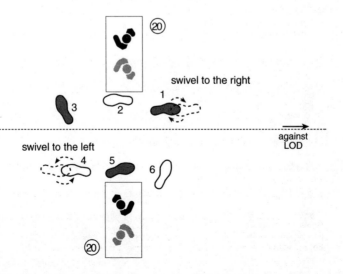

STEPS	**THE CLOSED BASIC**	BEATS

Start position (feet not illustrated). Normal hold.

Feet together, weight on LF. ***One**

  (backward half)

1 Q RF back onto ball of foot **Two**

2 Q Transfer weight forward onto LF **Three**

3 Close RF to LF **Four**

  S

3 Hold position ***One**

--------(forward half)--

4 Q LF forward with toes turned out **Two**

5 Q Transfer weight back onto RF **Three**

6 Close LF to RF **Four**

  S

6 Hold position ***One**

When you have mastered these steps, practise rotating the figure to the left.

Taking a side step on 3 and on 6 is another variant which, incidentally, **Two**

makes rotating the figure easier.

 Three

	THE PROGRESSIVE BASIC	Four

Start position (feet not illustrated). Normal hold.

Feet together, weight on LF. ***One**

  (backward half)

1 Q RF back onto ball of foot **Two**

2 Q Transfer weight forward onto LF **Three**

3 RF forward **Four**

  S

3 Hold position ***One**

------------------(forward half)---

4 Q LF forward with toes turned out **Two**

5 Q Transfer weight back onto RF **Three**

6 LF back **Four**

  S

6 Hold position ***One**

This figure is not rotated. Repeat as many times as you wish.

THE CLOSED BASIC

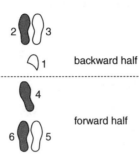

THE PROGRESSIVE BASIC

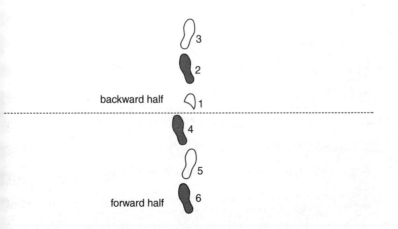

STEPS **SECOND POSITION BREAKS (CUCARACHAS)**   BEAT

Start position (feet illustrated). Normal hold. Feet together,
weight on LF.   *On

1 Q RF to the side with *part weight*   Tw

2 Q Transfer all weight sideways onto LF   Three

3 ● Close RF to LF   Fou

3 S Hold position   *On

---

4 Q LF to the side with *part weight*   Tw

5 Q Transfer all weight sideways onto RF   Three

6 ● Close LF to RF   Fou

6 S Hold position   *On

Repeat as many times as you wish. Follow with the Closed, The Progressive,
or the Turning Basic.   Tw

Three

CROSS-OVER BREAKS (THE NEW YORK)   Fou

Precede with the Closed Basic but step to the side on step 6.
Start position (feet not illustrated). Facing partner, feet apart, weight on LF,   *On
LH is released. RH is drawn forward leading you to turn.

1 Q Turn a quarter to the left. RF forward into RSP   Tw

2 Q Transfer weight back onto LF, start turning to the right   Three

3 ● RF to the side, turning right to face partner (DH)   Fou

3 S Hold position   *On

----------------LH is drawn forward leading you to turn. RH is released----------------

4 Q Turn a quarter to the right. LF forward into LSP   Tw

5 Q Transfer weight back onto RF, start turning to the left   Three

6 ● LF to the side, turning left to face partner (DH)   Fou

6 S Hold position   *On

Repeat as many times as you wish, then repeat steps 1–3 before following
with the Spot Turn to the right (as in the Cha-cha-cha and the Rumba).

SECOND POSITION BREAKS (CUCARACHAS)

4   6 5

also start
position

2 3   1

also start
position

CROSS-OVER BREAKS (THE NEW YORK)

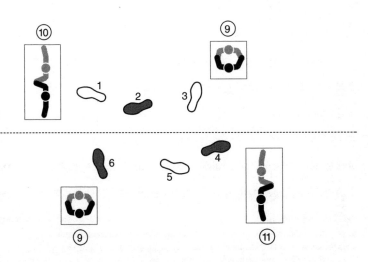

| **STEPS** | **THE BACK BREAK** | **BEAT** |

Start position (feet not illustrated). Normal or double hold.
Feet together, weight on LF.   *On*

1 Q RF back onto ball of foot   Tw

2 Q Transfer weight forward onto LF   Thre

3 RF a small step to the side of LF   Fou
S
3 Hold position   *On*

----

4 Q LF back onto ball of foot. (Partner also steps back)   Tw

5 Q Transfer weight forward onto RF   Three

6 Close LF to RF. (Return to start position)   Fou
S
6 Hold position   *On*

Repeat as many times as you wish. This figure is not rotated.
Follow with the Closed Basic, the Second Position Break or   Tw
the Double Back Break.
                                                                    Three

THE DOUBLE BACK BREAK   Fou

Start position (feet not illustrated). Normal or double hold.
Feet together, weight on LF.   *On*

1 Q RF back onto ball of foot. (Partner also steps back)   Tw

2 Q Transfer weight forward onto LF   Three

3 Close LF to RF. (Return to start position)   Fou
S
3 Hold position   *On*

----

4 Q LF back onto ball of foot. (Partner also steps back)   Tw

5 Q Transfer weight forward onto RF   Three

6 Close LF to RF. (Return to start position)   Fou
S
6 Hold position   *On*

As an alternative, steps 4, 5 and 6 may be danced turning right under raised
arms as in the Woman's Underarm Turn (Cha-cha-cha, Rumba). Follow with the
Closed, the Progressive, or the Turning Basic or with the Second Position Break.

THE BACK BREAK

THE DOUBLE BACK BREAK

STEPS	**THE TURNING BASIC**	BEATS
Start position (feet not illustrated). Facing centre in normal hold, weight on LF.		*One
1 Q RF back onto ball of foot		Two
2 Q Transfer weight forward onto LF		Three
3 RF forward, now in PP, still facing centre		Four
3 S Hold position		*One
4 Q LF a very small step forward pivoting for a half turn to the left		Two
5 Q Now facing wall, RF back and slightly to the side		Three
6 LF back. Return to start position. (Facing wall)		Four
6 S Hold position		*One
To make the turn comfortable, take small steps. As an easier alternative, on step 4, pivot only a quarter turn to face against LOD. Repeat as many times as you wish before following with the Closed Basic.		Two
		Three

	SPOT TURNS TO LEFT AND RIGHT	Four
Start position (feet not illustrated). Facing centre, feet apart, weight on LF (having stepped to the side on the previous step). LH is released. Your RH will be drawn in front of you to turn you and then released.		*One
1 Q Turn a quarter to the left. RF forward. (Facing against LOD)		Two
2 Q Transfer weight forward onto LF while turning to face LOD		Three
3 RF to side while completing a whole turn to face partner		Four
3 S Hold position		*One
4 Q Turn a quarter to the right. LF forward. (Facing LOD)		Two
5 Q Turn to face against LOD and transfer weight forward onto RF		Three
6 LF to side while completing a whole turn to face partner		Four
6 S Resume normal hold, then hold position		*One

The body movement initiates the turn. Keep the body braced and the steps small. Each turn may be danced separately. Follow with the Closed, the Progressive, or the Turning Basic.

THE TURNING BASIC

SPOT TURNS TO LEFT AND RIGHT

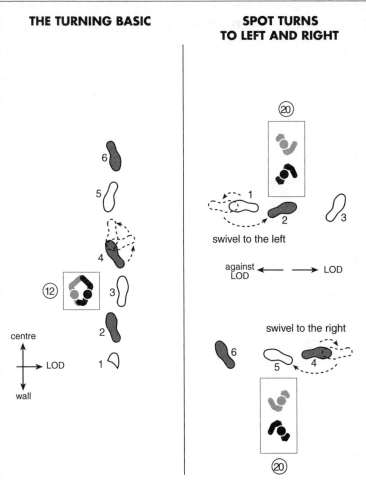

swivel to the left

against
LOD ← → LOD

swivel to the right

centre
↕
→ LOD
wall

Perfecting your Mambo technique

Starting

The first step of each figure may be danced on a bar's first or second beat (as shown) – whichever is emphasized. The musical emphasis varies and dancers interpret it differently. Be positive; step off and enjoy yourself.

Footwork

As in the Rumba, it is the ball of the stepping foot which first makes contact with the floor. This heel is lowered much more quickly, however, while the other heel lifts. Because the tempo is quick, the steps are small and the knees are never quite straight. The Mambo is characterized by an erect upper body with braced arms while, below the rib cage, the legs are in rapid, cushioned movement with the hips moving freely.

If the heel is lowered during a backward step, the lowering must be delayed if you and your partner are not to part company. The heel need not be lowered when you move back on step 1 or step 4 of a figure. The weight remains on the ball of the foot and there is a feeling of strong pressure. This is also felt with some side steps (in the Second Position Breaks, for example) and rocks when no transfer of weight occurs.

Arms

Arms are a little more curved than in the Rumba because partners dance closer to each other in normal hold and in one-hand hold figures such as the Cross Over Break. Certain figures, the Progressive Basic is one, are sometimes danced in double hold or with no hold. Dancers' free arms should move in sympathy with their steps. During Underarm Turns, arms are raised just high enough to clear the woman's head and then quickly lowered.

Partner's roles

The man is the choreographer. He must know his steps and lead his partner unhesitatingly yet gently from one figure to the next. The woman must follow his lead and avoid anticipating it.

Choreography

It is more satisfying to dance a few figures well than to attempt a long routine and forget *what comes next*.

The following figures in the Rumba chapter may be danced in a Mambo: The Hand to Hand, The Shoulder to Shoulder and the Alemana. Short, on-the-spot rock actions may be used to link these and other figures.

Alternative choreographies

a The Closed Basic.
Steps 1–3 of the Cross Over Break and 3 rocks in place (all repeated).
The Cross Over Breaks.
The Spot Turn to the Left (woman to right).

b Steps 1–3 of the Closed Basic.
Steps 4–6 of the Second Position Break.
Steps 1–3 of the Second Position Break.
Steps 4–6 of the Closed Basic.
The Shoulder to Shoulder (as in the Rumba).
The Woman's Underarm Turn to the Right.

c The Closed Basic.
The Turning Basic (twice).
The Closed Basic into the Woman's Underarm Turn to the Right.
Steps 1–6 of the Second Position Break (Cucarachas).
The Progressive Basic (twice) with the Woman's Underarm Turn to the Right for the last three steps.

d The Closed Basic.
The Back Break.
The Double Back Break with the Woman's Underarm Turn to the Right – *take double hold for* – The Fifth Position Break (the Hand to Hand, as in the Rumba).
The Spot Turn to the Left (woman to the right).

5 | SAMBA

The ancestor of what we now call the Samba was brought to the state of Bahia in north-east Brazil at the beginning of the eighteenth century by African slaves. There the slaves mingled with indigenous Indians, worked with them on plantations and, when there was something to celebrate, danced with them.

Three generations on, the ritual dance the slaves had introduced had lost much of its tribal symbolism, had gained steps from the Indians' dances, especially the Maxixe, and had become the most popular street dance at carnivals. It reached Rio de Janeiro, a thousand miles away, during the nineteenth century and was adopted as Brazil's national dance.

The filmed story of the American dancers, Irene and Vernon Castle, (which featured Fred Astaire and Ginger Rogers) broadcasting and Brazil's own Carmen Miranda have given the Samba to the world.

The Samba's music, in 2/4 time, (two beats to each bar) with a tempo of 48–56 bars per minute, conveys the busy, carnival atmosphere of the dance which, appropriately for a street dance, includes many travelling figures in which couples progress anti-clockwise around the ballroom. The characteristic Samba bounce is what makes it a busy, lively dance, but the basic steps are easy to learn.

Bounce action

When dancing the three Basic Bounce Action figures on pages 74–75 (men) and 84–85 (women), you take two steps during each two-beat bar of music which is counted *one-two* or *slow-slow*. When you dance the other Alternative Bounce Action figures, you take three steps during each two-beat bar which is counted *one-a-two* or *slow-a-slow.* The time values for these three steps are $3/4$; $1/4$; 1. The $1/4$ beat is shown as *a* in the beat column.

Holds

The normal hold position is the same as the Rumba's but several figures are danced in promenade and other hold positions.

Footwork

Footwork to be ball flat except when steps are taken between beats.

Figure 5.1   Normal hold position

STEPS	**THE NATURAL BASIC MOVEMENT** **using Basic Bounce Action**	BEATS
	Start position (feet illustrated). Normal hold. Feet together. Weight on LF. (forward half)	Two
1	RF forward	*One
2	Close LF to RF with pressure but without change of weight	Two
	(backward half)	
3	LF back	*One
4	Close RF to LF with pressure but without change of weight	Two

This figure may be rotated a quarter turn or more to the right.
Repeat as you wish.

*One

Two

THE NATURAL BASIC MOVEMENT
using Alternative Bounce Action

*One

Two

Start position (feet illustrated). Normal hold. Feet together. Weight on LF. (forward half)

1	RF forward	*One
2	Close LF to RF rising to balls of feet	a
3	Replace weight onto RF	Two
	(backward half)	
4	LF back	*One
5	Close RF to LF rising to balls of feet	a
6	Replace weight onto LF	Two

This figure may be rotated a quarter turn or more to the right.
Repeat as you wish.

*One

Two

THE REVERSE BASIC MOVEMENT
using Basic Bounce Action

*One

Start position (feet illustrated). Normal hold. Feet together. Weight on RF. (forward half)

Two

1	LF forward	*One
2	Close RF to LF with pressure but without change of weight	Two
	(backward half)	
3	RF back	*One
4	Close LF to RF with pressure but without change of weight	Two

This figure may be rotated a quarter turn or more to the left.
Repeat as you wish. (This figure may also be danced using Alternative
Bounce Action.)

THE NATURAL BASIC MOVEMENT
using Basic Bounce Action

also start position

THE NATURAL BASIC MOVEMENT
using Alternative Bounce Action

also start position

THE REVERSE BASIC MOVEMENT
using Basic Bounce Action

also start position

STEPS	**THE PROGRESSIVE BASIC MOVEMENT**	BEATS
	using Slight Basic Bounce Action	

Start position (feet illustrated). Normal hold. Feet together.   **Two**
Weight on LF (facing DW). Precede with the Natural Basic Movement.

1	RF forward	*One

2	Close LF to RF with pressure but without change of weight	Two

3	LF to side	*One

4	Close RF to LF with pressure but without change of weight	Two

This figure is not rotated. Repeat as you wish.
Follow with the Natural Basic Movement or the Whisk   ***One**
to the Right.

Two

THE WHISK TO THE LEFT AND RIGHT   ***One**
using Alternative Bounce Action

Precede with a Basic Movement. Start position (feet illustrated).
Normal hold. Feet together. Weight on RF. (Facing wall.)   **Two**
   (to the left)

1	LF to side	*One
2	Place ball of RF, with toe turned out, behind heel of LF	a
3	Replace weight onto LF	Two

   (to the right)

4	RF to side	*One
5	Place ball of LF with toe turned out, behind heel of RF	a
6	Replace weight onto RF	Two

Follow with the Basic Movement or the Rhythm Bounce or turn
left into PP during steps 4–6 for the Samba Walks (below).   ***One**

Two

THE SAMBA WALKS   ***One**
using Slight Alternative Bounce Action

Start position (feet not illustrated). PP. Weight on RF. (Facing LOD.)   **Two**

1	LF forward, moving along LOD	*One
2	RF a small step back (on ball) with a straight knee and part-weight	a
3	Draw LF slightly back towards RF	Two

4	RF forward in PP, moving along LOD	*One
5	LF a small step back (on ball) with a straight knee and part-weight	a
6	Draw RF slightly back towards LF	Two

Slight Bounce Action coupled with the movement of the feet results in a forward
and backward swing of the hips. Follow with a Whisk to the Left in which you
turn right to face your partner on the first step.

THE PROGRESSIVE BASIC MOVEMENT
using Slight Basic Bounce Action
(travelling DW)

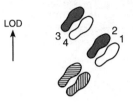

THE WHISK TO THE LEFT AND RIGHT
using Alternative Bounce Action

(to the left)

(to the right)

THE SAMBA WALKS
using Slight Alternative Bounce Action

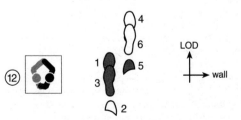

STEPS	**THE RHYTHM BOUNCE**	BEATS
	using Alternative Bounce Action	

Precede with a Whisk to the Right. Start position (feet illustrated) facing partner.   **Two**
Normal or one-hand hold. Weight on RF. (Facing wall.)

1	LF to side and slightly back with right heel released	*One
2	With feet in place, swing hips to the right	a
3	With feet in place, swing hips to the left	Two
4	With feet in place, swing hips to the right	a
5	With feet in place, swing hips to the left	*One
6	With feet in place, swing hips to the right	a
7	With feet in place, swing hips to the left	Two

Right knee inclines forwards left throughout. Follow with the
Simple Volta (travelling left).   *One

                                                                                         Two

THE SIMPLE VOLTA (travelling left)
using Alternative Bounce Action.   *One

Precede with the Rhythm Bounce. Start position (feet illustrated) facing partner.
Normal or one-hand hold. Weight on LF. (Facing wall.)   Two
(Moving sideways to the left along LOD.)

1	Place RF, with toe turned out, in front of LF	*One
2	Place ball of LF to side and slightly back with toe turned out	a
3	Slide RF, with toe turned out, in front of LF	Two
4	Place ball of LF to side and slightly back with toe turned out	a
5	Slide RF, with toe turned out, in front of LF	*One
6	Place ball of LF to side and slightly back with toe turned out	a
7	Slide RF, with toe turned out, in front of LF	Two

Follow with a Whisk to your Left or with the Spot Volta (overleaf).
To dance the Simple Volta (travelling right) commence by placing LF,   *One
with toe turned out, in front of RF on step 1.

                                                                                         Two

THE SOLO SPOT VOLTA
using Alternative Bounce Action   *One

Start position (feet illustrated) facing partner. Normal or
one-hand hold. Weight on RF. (Facing wall.) Lead by turning   Two
your partner to her right with your LH, then release hold.

1	Turn left to face LOD placing LF with toe turned out in front of RF	*One
2	Still turning RF to side and slightly back rising to balls of feet	a
3	Replace LF, with toe turned out, in front of RF	Two

(Having completed a whole turn to face partner.)
The ball of the LF remains on the spot between steps 2 and 3 while you turn to your
left (partner to right). Resume normal hold and follow with a Whisk to the Right.
You may also repeat steps 2 and 3 twice, (seven steps in all) making a *total* of
one or two turns while dancing to a *1a2a3a4* rhythm, as illustrated.

THE RHYTHM BOUNCE
using Alternative Bounce Action

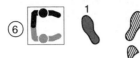

start position after Whisk

THE SIMPLE VOLTA (travelling left)
using Alternative Bounce Action

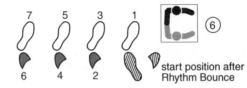

start position after
Rhythm Bounce

THE SOLO SPOT VOLTA
using Alternative Bounce Action

(rhythm 1a2)   (rhythm 1a2a3a4)   wall

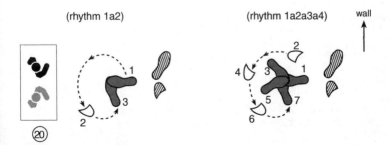

STEPS	**THE SPOT VOLTA TO THE RIGHT**	BEATS
	using Alternative Bounce Action	

Precede with the Whisk to the Right or with the Simple Volta | Two
(travelling left). Start position (feet illustrated) facing partner.
Normal or one-hand hold. Weight on RF. (Facing wall.) | *One
Your steps are the same as the Whisk to the left, but you
turn your partner to her right under your LH | Two

1	LF to side, raise LH. Turn partner to her right and release RH	*One
2	Place ball of RF, with toe turned out, behind heel of LF	a
3	Replace weight onto LF. Resume normal hold	Two

Follow with the Whisk to the Right or with the Natural Basic Movement.
To dance the Spot Volta to the Left, dance a Whisk to the Right while turning your | *One
partner to her left under your raised LH. Follow this with the Whisk to the Left or
with the Reverse Basic Movement. | Two

| | | *One |
| | | Two |

| | **THE REVERSE TURN** | *One |
| | **using Alternative Bounce Action** | |

Precede with the Reverse Basic Movement ending facing DC. | Two
Start position (feet illustrated). Close normal hold. Feet together. Weight on RF.

1	LF forward. Start turning to the left	*One
2	Still turning, RF (on ball) to the side and slightly back	a
3	Still turning, cross LF, with toe turned out, in front of RF	Two
	(to face against LOD)	
4	Still turning, RF back and slightly to the right	*One
5	Still turning, close left heel to right heel	a
6	Close RF to LF, completing seven-eighths of a turn, to face LOD	Two

To facilitate turning, keep the steps small and the hold close. Follow with another
Reverse Turn, the Reverse Basic Movement, the Whisk to the Left or with the
Bota Fogos (overleaf). This figure may be started facing LOD and finished facing DW.
It may also be under-turned slightly.

THE SPOT VOLTA TO THE RIGHT
using Alternative Bounce Action

start position after dancing the Simple Volta

THE REVERSE TURN
using Alternative Bounce Action

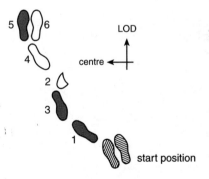

STEPS	**THE BOTA FOGOS IN PP AND CPP**	BEATS
	using Alternative Bounce Action	

Precede with the Reverse Basic or with the Reverse Turn. ***One**

Start position (feet not illustrated). Normal hold.

Feet together. Weight on RF. (Facing wall.) **Two**

1	LF forward. (Partner back)	***One**
2	Place ball of RF to side with part-weight	**a**
3	Release LF momentarily; replace it having turned to face DW	**Two**
	(Now in PP)	
4	RF forward and slightly across LF (in PP) moving along LOD	***One**
5	Turning right to face partner, place ball of LF to side with part-weight	**a**
6	Release RF momentarily; replace it having turned into CPP	**Two**
	(facing DW against LOD)	
7	LF forward and slightly across RF (in CPP) moving against LOD	***One**
8	Turning left to face partner, place ball of RF to side with part-weight	**a**
9	Release LF momentarily; replace it having turned to face DW	**Two**
	(Now in PP)	

To facilitate turning from PP to CPP, relax your hold while maintaining the ***One**
correct body position. Steps 4–9 may be repeated. Follow with the Samba
Walks starting with step 4. A simpler way to start the Bota Fogos is to **Two**
dance an LF Samba Walk in PP instead of steps 1, 2 and 3 above.

*One

Two

THE STATIONARY SAMBA WALKS
using Slight Alternative Bounce Action ***One**

Precede with the Simple Volta (travelling Left). Start position
(feet not illustrated) facing partner. Normal or one-hand hold. **Two**
Weight on RF. (Facing wall.)

1	Close LF to RF	***One**
2	RF back (on ball) with a straight knee and part-weight	**a**
3	Draw LF slightly back towards RF	**Two**
4	Close RF slightly forward of LF	***One**
5	LF back (on ball) with a straight knee and part-weight	**a**
6	Draw RF slightly back towards LF	**Two**

Follow with the Spot Volta to the Right or with the Solo Spot Volta.

THE BOTA FOGOS IN PP AND CPP
using Alternative Bounce Action

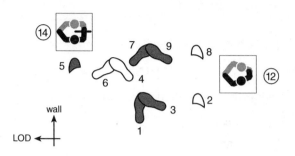

THE STATIONARY SAMBA WALKS
using Slight Alternative Bounce Action

STEPS	**THE NATURAL BASIC MOVEMENT** **using Basic Bounce Action**	BEATS
	Start position (feet illustrated). Normal hold. Feet together. Weight on RF. (backward half)	Two
1	LF back	*One
2	Close RF to LF with pressure but without change of weight	Two
	(forward half)	
3	RF forward	*One
4	Close LF to RF with pressure but without change of weight	Two

This figure may be rotated a quarter turn or more to the right.
Repeat as you wish.

*One

Two

THE NATURAL BASIC MOVEMENT
using Alternative Bounce Action

*One

Two

Start position (feet illustrated). Normal hold. Feet together. Weight on RF.
(backward half)

1	LF back	*One
2	Close RF to LF rising to balls of feet	a
3	Replace weight onto LF	Two
	(forward half)	
4	RF forward	*One
5	Close LF to RF rising to balls of feet	a
6	Replace weight onto RF	Two

This figure may be rotated a quarter turn or more to the right.
Repeat as you wish.

*One

Two

THE REVERSE BASIC MOVEMENT
using Basic Bounce Action

*One

Start position (feet illustrated). Normal hold. Feet together. Weight on LF.
(backward half)

Two

1	RF back	*One
2	Close LF to RF with pressure but without change of weight	Two
	(forward half)	
3	LF forward	*One
4	Close RF to LF with pressure but without change of weight	Two

This figure may be rotated a quarter turn or more to the left. Repeat as you wish.
(This figure may also be danced using Alternative Bounce Action.)

THE NATURAL BASIC MOVEMENT
using Basic Bounce Action

also start position

THE NATURAL BASIC MOVEMENT
using Alternative Bounce Action

also start position

THE REVERSE BASIC MOVEMENT
using Basic Bounce Action

also start position

STEPS	**THE PROGRESSIVE BASIC MOVEMENT**	BEATS
	using Slight Basic Bounce Action	

Start position (feet illustrated) facing partner. Normal hold. Feet together. Weight on RF (facing DC against LOD). Precede with the Natural Basic Movement. — **Two**

1	LF back	*One

2	Close RF to LF with pressure but without change of weight	Two

3	RF to side	*One

4	Close LF to RF with pressure but without change of weight	Two

This figure is not rotated. Repeat as you wish.
Follow with the Natural Basic Movement or the Whisk to the Left. — ***One**

Two

THE WHISK TO THE RIGHT AND LEFT
using Alternative Bounce Action

*One

Precede with a Basic Movement. Start position (feet illustrated) facing partner.
Normal hold. Feet together. Weight on LF. (Facing centre.) — **Two**

(to the right)

1	RF to side	*One
2	Place ball of LF, with toe turned out, behind heel of RF	a
3	Replace weight onto RF	Two

(to the left)

4	LF to side	*One
5	Place ball of RF, with toe turned out, behind heel of LF	a
6	Replace weight onto LF	Two

Follow with the Basic Movement or the Rhythm Bounce or turn
right into PP during steps 4–6 for the Samba Walks (below). — ***One**

Two

*One

THE SAMBA WALKS
using Slight Alternative Bounce Action

Two

Start position (feet not illustrated). PP. Weight on LF. (Facing LOD.)

1	RF forward, moving along LOD	*One
2	LF a small step back (on ball) with a straight knee and part weight	a
3	Draw RF slightly back towards LF	Two

4	LF forward in PP, moving along LOD	*One
5	RF a small step back (on ball) with a straight knee and part weight	a
6	Draw LF slightly back towards RF	Two

Slight Bounce Action coupled with the movement of the feet results in a forward
and backward swing of the hips. Follow with a Whisk to the Right in which you
turn left to face your partner on the first step.

THE PROGRESSIVE BASIC MOVEMENT
using Slight Basic Bounce Action
(facing DC against LOD)

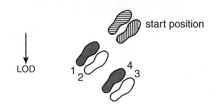

start position

LOD

1 2 4 3

THE WHISK TO THE RIGHT AND LEFT
using Alternative Bounce Action

(to the right)

start position

1 & 3 2

(to the left)

4 & 6 5

start position

THE SAMBA WALKS
using Slight Alternative Bounce Action

LOD

centre

4 6 5 1 3 2

(12)

STEPS	**THE RHYTHM BOUNCE**	BEATS
	using Alternative Bounce Action	

Precede with a Whisk to the Left. Start position (feet illustrated)   **Two**
facing partner. Normal or one-hand hold. Weight on RF. (Facing centre.)

1	RF to side and slightly back with left heel released	*One
2	With feet in place, swing hips to the left	a
3	With feet in place, swing hips to the right	Two
4	With feet in place, swing hips to the left	a
5	With feet in place, swing hips to the right	*One
6	With feet in place, swing hips to the left	a
7	With feet in place, swing hips to the right	Two

Left knee inclines towards right knee throughout.
Follow with the Simple Volta (travelling right).   ***One**

THE SIMPLE VOLTA (travelling right)   Two
using Alternative Bounce Action

Precede with the Rhythm Bounce.   ***One**
Start position (feet illustrated) facing partner. Normal or one-hand hold.
Weight on RF. (Facing centre.)   **Two**
(Moving sideways to the right along LOD.)

1	Place LF, with toe turned out, in front of RF	*One
2	Place ball of RF to side and slightly back with toe turned out	a
3	Slide LF, with toe turned out, in front of RF	Two
4	Place ball of RF to side and slightly back with toe turned out	a
5	Slide LF, with toe turned out, in front of RF	*One
6	Place ball of RF to side and slightly back with toe turned out	a
7	Slide LF, with toe turned out, in front of RF	Two

Follow with a Whisk to the Right or with the Spot Volta (overleaf).
To dance the Simple Volta (travelling left) commence by placing RF,   ***One**
with toe turned out, in front of LF on step 1.

Two

THE SOLO SPOT VOLTA   *One
using Alternative Bounce Action

Start position (feet illustrated) facing partner. Normal or   **Two**
one-hand hold. Weight on LF. (Facing centre.) You will be
led to turn to your right. Your hand will then be released.

1	Turn right to face LOD placing RF with toe turned out, in front of LF	*One
2	Still turning, LF to side and slightly back rising to balls of feet	a
3	Replace RF, with toe turned out, in front of LF	Two

(Having completed a whole turn to face partner)
The ball of the RF remains on the spot between steps 2 and 3 while you turn
to your right (partner turns left). Resume normal hold and follow with a Whisk
to the Left. You may also repeat steps 2 and 3 twice, (seven steps in all) making
a *total* of one or two turns while dancing to a *1a2a3a4* rhythm, as illustrated.

THE RHYTHM BOUNCE
using Alternative Bounce Action

THE SIMPLE VOLTA (travelling left)
using Alternative Bounce Action

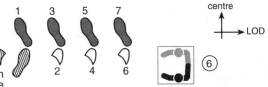

start position
after Rhythm Bounce

centre → LOD

THE SOLO SPOT VOLTA
using Alternative Bounce Action

(rhythm 1a 2a 3a 4)   (rhythm 1a 2)

centre

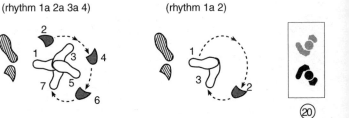

STEPS		BEATS
THE SPOT VOLTA TO THE RIGHT **using Alternative Bounce Action**		
Precede with the Whisk to the Left or with the Simple Volta		*One
(travelling right). Start position (feet illustrated) facing partner.		
Normal or one-hand hold. Weight on LF. (Facing centre.) RH is raised.		Two

1	Turn right to face LOD placing RF, with toe turned out, in front of LF	*One
2	Still turning, LF to side and slightly back rising to balls of feet	a
3	Replace RF, with toe turned out, in front of LF	Two

(Having completed a whole turn to face partner)

	BEATS
The ball of the RF remains on the spot between steps 2 and 3. Resume	*One
normal hold and follow with a Whisk to the Left or with the Natural	
Basic Movement. The Spot Volta may also be danced starting	Two
with your LF and turning to your left under a raised RH. Follow	
with the Whisk to the Right or with the Reverse Basic Movement.	*One
	Two

THE REVERSE TURN **using Alternative Bounce Action**		*One
Precede with the Reverse Basic Movement ending facing DW against LOD.		Two
Start position (feet illustrated). Normal hold. Feet together. Weight on LF.		

1	RF back. Start turning left	*One
2	Still turning, close left heel to right heel	a
3	Still turning, close RF to LF to face LOD	Two

4	Still turning, LF forward	*One
5	Still turning, RF (on ball) to the side and slightly back	a
6	Cross LF, with toe turned out, in front of RF	Two

(Having completed a seven-eighths turn to face against LOD)

To facilitate turning, keep the steps small and the hold closer than usual.
Follow with another Reverse Turn, the Reverse Basic Movement, the Whisk
to the Right or with the Bota Fogos (overleaf). This figure may be started
facing against LOD and finished facing DC against LOD. It may also be
under-turned slightly.

THE SPOT VOLTA TO THE RIGHT
using Alternative Bounce Action

start position
after dancing the Simple Volta

THE REVERSE TURN
using Alternative Bounce Action

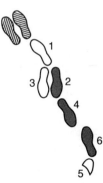

STEPS	**THE BOTA FOGOS IN PP AND CPP**	BEATS
	using Alternative Bounce Action	
	Precede with the Reverse Basic or with the Reverse Turn.	*One
	Start position (feet not illustrated) facing partner. Normal hold.	
	Feet together (or crossed). Weight on LF. (Facing centre.)	Two

1	RF back	*One
2	Place ball of LF to side with part weight	a
3	Release RF momentarily; replace it having turned to face DC.	Two
	(Now in PP)	
4	LF forward and slightly across RF (in PP) moving along LOD	*One
5	Turning left to face partner, place ball of RF to side with part weight	a
6	Release LF momentarily; replace it having turned into CPP	Two
	(Facing DC against LOD)	
7	RF forward and slightly across LF (in CPP) moving against LOD	*One
8	Turning right to face partner, place ball of LF to side with part weight	a
9	Release RF momentarily; replace it having turned to face DC	Two
	(Now in PP)	

To facilitate turning from PP to CPP, the hold should be relaxed		*One
while maintaining the correct body position. Steps 4–9 may be repeated.		
Follow with the Samba Walks starting with step 4.		Two
A simpler way to start the Bota Fogos is to dance an RF Samba Walk		
in PP instead of steps 1, 2 and 3 above.		*One
		Two

	THE STATIONARY SAMBA WALKS	
	using Slight Alternative Bounce Action	*One
	Precede with the Simple Volta (travelling right). Start position	
	(feet not illustrated) facing partner. Normal or one-hand hold.	Two
	Weight on LF. (Facing centre.)	
1	Close RF to LF	*One
2	LF back (on ball) with a straight knee and part weight	a
3	Draw RF slightly back towards LF	Two

4	Close LF slightly forward of RF	*One
5	RF back (on ball) with a straight knee and part weight	a
6	Draw LF slightly back towards RF	Two

Follow with the Spot Volta to the Right or with the Solo Spot Volta.

THE BOTA FOGOS IN PP AND CPP
using Alternative Bounce Action

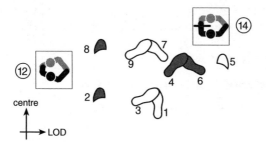

centre

→ LOD

THE STATIONARY SAMBA WALKS
using Slight Alternative Bounce Action

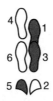

Perfecting your Samba technique

Starting

Although there are two beats to each bar, the musical phrasing often suggests that bars are linked – an impression reinforced by dance teachers who usually continue to count *one-two-three-four* or *one-a-two-a-three-a-four* throughout the dance. This helps students to step off on the following beat *one*. The music has a strong beat which makes starting easy.

Footwork and the Samba Bounce

When you dance Basic Bounce Action figures – the Natural Basic, the Reverse Basic and the Progressive Basic – you step forward or back *ball flat*, with flexed knees, on beat one. Your knees then straighten slightly before flexing once more as your other foot closes *ball flat* with *pressure* – but without transferring weight – on beat two. Again your knees straighten slightly before flexing once more for the following beat one.

The only difference when you dance Alternative Bounce Action figures is that you take a between-beat step on the ball of your foot, with straightened knees on the *-a-* count.

The straightening and flexing of your knees which causes your poised upper body and braced arms to rise and fall continually, gives the Samba its characteristic bounce or *tick*.

When you take a step with *part weight* (Bota Fogos) you transfer your weight only for an instant.

Arms

When you dance one-hand hold figures, your free arm is extended in a gentle curve with your hand held palm down at about your waist level.

Partner's roles

The man must choreograph the dance and lead his partner into each figure, making sure they face in the right direction to go with the flow, anti-clockwise around the floor. To match the musical phrasing, it helps to count steps in groups of four – see **Alternative choreographies**.

Alternative choreographies

a 2 Natural Basic Movement.
2 Progress Basic Movement.
2 Natural Basic Movement
(to face wall).
3 Whisks.
Spot Volta to Right.

b (Start with LF.)
4 Whisks (finish in PP).
4 Samba Walks in PP.
2 Whisks.
Rhythm Bounce.
Simple Volta to Left
(woman's right).
Spot Volta to Right.
Whisk to the Right
(woman's left).

c (Start with LF.)
2 Whisks.
Solo Spot Volta to Left
(womans right) using the
rhythm *1a2a3a4*.
2 Stationary Samba Walks.
Solo Spot Volta to Right
(woman's left) using the
rhythm *1a2a3a4*.

d Reverse Turn.
Reverse Basic Movement.
Reverse Turn (to face wall).
2 Whisks.
2 Stationary Samba Walks.
Spot Volta to Right.
Whisk to Right (woman's
left).

e 3 Samba Walks in PP.
4 Bota Fogos (start RF,
woman LF).
3 Samba Walks in PP (man
RF, woman LF).
Solo Spot Volta to Left
(woman's right).
2 Whisks.
Solo Spot Volta to Right
(woman's left).
2 Whisks.

f 2 Reverse Turns (to face
wall).
Bota Fogos.
3 Samba Walks in PP.
2 Whisks.
Spot Volta to Right.
Whisk to Right (woman's
left).

6 | BOSSA NOVA

The music of the Bossa Nova (*New Trend* in Portuguese) has been popular since the 1930s, and several early recordings, such as *Fly me to the Moon* and *Blame it on the Bossa Nova*, were hits in their time. The unmistakable Bossa Nova beat still characterizes many of the numbers in today's charts – so why hasn't this easy dance, whose steps so neatly mirror its rhythm, caught on like its Brazilian ancestor, the Samba?

Bossa Nova music is in 4/4 time (four beats to each bar) and has a tempo which ranges from 27 bars per minute for *Baion* music to 50 bars per minute for *authentic* Bossa Nova music. Three steps are danced during each bar – the first *slow* step being taken over the first two beats of the *slow-quick-quick* rhythm.

Although the step pattern resembles the Samba's, that dance's *bounce* is replaced by a Rumba-style *hip swing* which gives to the Bossa Nova a sensuous, seductive appeal, especially when its tempo is slow.

Practise the Basic Movement, the Side Basic and the Cross Basic on the following pages until you can respond to the rhythm without thinking about your feet. These figures should be mastered before anything else is attempted because they form the framework into which other figures fit.

Holds

Until the 1970s, the Bossa Nova was usually treated as a *challenge dance* by couples who danced facing, but a little apart from, each other without hold. The man would start a figure which his partner then attempted to follow with only occasional, fleeting hand holds. Because the contemporary *Twist* was a much easier challenge dance, Bossa Nova dancers gradually gave up the challenge and became more companionable – so that today the normal hold position is the same as the Rumba's. Other holds, especially one-hand hold (the man's left holding the woman's right), are often used but some figures are still frequently danced without hold.

Footwork

Footwork to be ball flat unless instructed otherwise.

Figure 6.1   Normal hold position

STEPS	THE BASIC MOVEMENT	BEATS
	Start position (feet illustrated) facing partner. Feet together.	
	Weight on RF. Normal/double/one-hand/ without hold. (Facing wall.)	Four
	(forward half)	
1 S	LF forward leaving right leg extended and heel released	*One
1	Hold position	Two
2 Q	Close RF to LF	Three
3 Q	Transfer weight onto LF	Four
	----------------(backward half)---	
4 S	RF back leaving left leg extended and heel released	*One
4	Hold position	Two
5 Q	Close LF to RF	Three
6 Q	Transfer weight onto RF	Four
	Repeat as you wish.	
		*One
		Two

	THE CROSS BASIC	Three
	Start position (feet illustrated) facing partner.	
	Feet together. Weight on RF. Normal/double/one-hand/without hold.	
	(Facing wall.)	Four
	(to the left)	
1 S	LF to the side leaving right leg extended and heel released	*One
1	Hold position	Two
2 Q	Cross RF on ball of foot behind LF	Three
3 Q	Transfer weight onto LF	Four
	(to the right)	
4 S	RF to the side leaving left leg extended and heel released	*One
4	Hold position	Two
5 Q	Cross LF on ball of foot behind RF	Three
6 Q	Transfer weight onto RF	Four

Repeat as you wish. If you close your feet (instead of crossing them) on steps
2 and 5, the figure is then called The **Side Basic** (illustrated opposite).

THE BASIC MOVEMENT

 forward half

---

backward half

also start position

THE CROSS BASIC

(to the left)   (to the right)

start positions

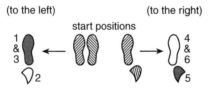

THE SIDE BASIC

(to the left)   (to the right)

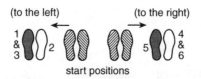

start positions

STEPS	**THE SOLO TURN (to the left) into**	BEATS
	THE SIDE BASIC (to the right)	

Start position (feet not illustrated) facing partner. Feet together | Three
Weight on RF. Normal/double/one-hand/without hold. (Facing wall.)

Four

| **1** S | LF to side along LOD in PP starting to turn left | *One |
| **1** | Hold position | Two |

| **2** Q | RF forward to face LOD. Turn partner right. Release hold | Three |

| **3** Q | Swivel on both feet a half turn to the left. Weight on to LF | Four |

| **4** S | Complete a whole left turn to face partner. RF to the side | *One |
| **4** | Hold position (leaving left leg extended) | Two |

| **5** Q | Close LF to RF | Three |

| **6** Q | Transfer weight onto RF, resuming any hold | Four |

These steps may be repeated. The Solo Turn may be turned to the right and
followed with the Side Basic to the left, (these steps are not shown). | *One

Two

THE PUSH AWAY

Start position (feet illustrated) facing partner. Feet together. | Three
Weight on RF. Normal/double/one-hand/without hold. (Facing wall.)
(Push partner away gently, retaining LH hold while releasing RH.) | Four

| **1** S | LF back leaving right leg extended and heel released | *One |
| **1** | Hold position | Two |

| **2** Q | Close RF to LF | Three |

3 Q	Transfer weight onto LF	Four
	(Gently pull partner towards you)	
4 S	RF forward leaving left leg extended and heel released	*One
4	Hold position	Two

| **5** Q | Close LF to RF | Three |

| **6** Q | Transfer weight onto RF. Resume hold | Four |

These steps may be repeated.

THE SOLO TURN (to the left) into
THE SIDE BASIC (to the right)

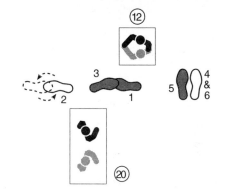

THE PUSH AWAY

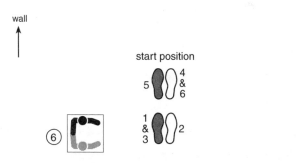

STEPS	**THE FACE TO FACE AND BACK TO BACK**	BEATS

Start position (feet illustrated) facing partner. Feet together.
Weight on RF. Normal/double/one-hand hold. (Facing wall.)   **Four**
Turn left, leading partner to turn right. Release hold.

1 S Facing LOD, LF forward   ***One**

1 Hold position   **Two**

2 Q Continue turning left to face centre, RF a small step to side   **Three**

3 Q Close LF to RF. (Now back to back with your partner)   **Four**

4 S Turn right to face LOD, RF forward   ***One**

4 Hold position   **Two**

5 Q Continue turning right to face wall, LF a small step to side   **Three**

6 Q Close RF to LF. (Now facing partner again)   **Four**
Repeat these six steps, then resume any hold and continue with
the Basic Movement.   ***One**

                                                                            Two

THE PROMENADE ROCK   **Three**

Precede with the Cross Basic to the Right turning left into PP as illustrated
opposite. (Facing LOD.) Start position (feet not illustrated).   **Four**
Weight on RF.

1 S LF forward still facing LOD   ***One**

1 Hold position   **Two**

2 Q Rock back onto RF (Fallaway Position)   **Three**

3 Q Rock forward onto LF (in PP)   **Four**

4 S RF forward and across (still in PP), start turning right   ***One**

4 Hold position   **Two**

5 Q Turn right to face partner. LF to the side   **Three**

6 Q Close RF to LF   **Four**
As an alternative, you may dance steps 1–3 three times with alternate feet
(starting with LF the first time) before dancing steps 4–6 thus extending the
figure during two more bars of music. Follow with any other Bossa Nova figure.

THE FACE TO FACE AND BACK TO BACK

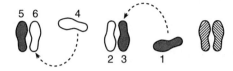

THE CROSS BASIC TO THE RIGHT
(turning left into PP)

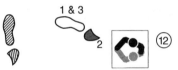

THE PROMENADE ROCK

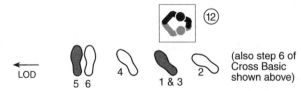

(also step 6 of
Cross Basic
shown above)

STEPS	**THE BASIC MOVEMENT**	BEATS

Start position (feet illustrated) facing partner. Feet together. Weight on LF.

Normal/double/one-hand/without hold. (Facing centre.)   **Four**

(backward half)

1 S	RF back leaving left leg extended and heel released	*One
1	Hold position	Two
2 Q	Close LF to RF	Three
3 Q	Transfer weight onto RF	Four

----------------(forward half)--

4 S	LF forward leaving right leg extended and heel released	*One
4	Hold position	Two
5 Q	Close RF to LF	Three
6 Q	Transfer weight onto LF	Four

Repeat as you wish.

                                                    *One

                                                    Two

THE CROSS BASIC

Start position (feet illustrated) facing partner. Feet together.   **Three**

Weight on LF. Normal/double/one-hand/without hold.

(Facing centre.)   **Four**

(to the right)

1 S	RF to the side leaving left leg extended and heel released	*One
1	Hold position	Two
2 Q	Cross LF on ball of foot behind RF	Three
3 Q	Transfer weight onto RF	Four

(to the left)

4 S	LF to the side leaving right leg extended and heel released	*One
4	Hold position	Two
5 Q	Cross RF on ball of foot behind LF	Three
6 Q	Transfer weight onto LF	Four

Repeat as you wish. If you close your feet (instead of crossing them) on steps 2 and 5, the figure is then called The **Side Basic** (illustrated opposite).

THE BASIC MOVEMENT

also start position

forward half

---

backward half

THE CROSS BASIC

(to the left)   (to the right)

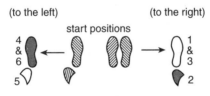

THE SIDE BASIC

(to the left)   (to the right)

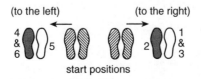

STEPS	**THE SOLO TURN (to the right) into THE SIDE BASIC (to the left)**	BEATS

Start position (feet not illustrated) facing partner. Feet together.
Weight on LF. Normal/double/one-hand/without hold. (Facing centre.)

Three

Four

1 **S**	RF to side along LOD in PP starting to turn right	*One
1 **S**	Hold position	Two

| 2 | Q | LF forward, turning to face LOD. Partner turns left. Hold released | Three |

| 3 | Q | Swivel on both feet a half turn to the right. Weight on to RF | Four |

4 **S**	Complete a whole right turn to face partner. LF to the side	*One
4 **S**	Hold position (leaving right leg extended)	Two

| 5 | Q | Close RF to LF | Three |

| 6 | Q | Transfer weight onto LF, resuming any hold | Four |

These steps may be repeated. The Solo Turn may be turned to the left and
followed with the Side Basic to the right (these steps are not shown).

*One

Two

THE PUSH AWAY

Start position (feet illustrated) facing partner. Feet together.
Weight on LF. Normal/double/one-hand/hold. (Facing centre.)

Three

Four

(You are pushed backwards. Release LH. RH still held.)

1 **S**	RF back leaving left leg extended and heel released	*One
1 **S**	Hold position	Two

| 2 | Q | Close LF to RF | Three |

| 3 | Q | Transfer weight onto RF | Four |

(You are pulled towards your partner)

4 **S**	LF forward leaving right leg extended and heel released	*One
4 **S**	Hold position	Two

| 5 | Q | Close RF to LF | Three |

| 6 | Q | Transfer weight onto LF. Resume hold | Four |

These steps may be repeated.

THE SOLO TURN (to the right) into
THE SIDE BASIC (to the left)

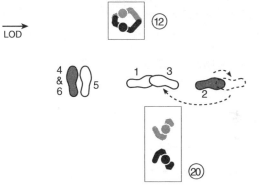

LOD

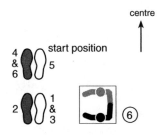

THE PUSH AWAY

centre

STEPS	**THE FACE TO FACE AND BACK TO BACK**	BEATS

Start position (feet illustrated) facing partner. Feet together.
Weight on LF. Normal/double/one-hand hold. (Facing centre.) **Four**
Turn right, while your partner turns left. Hold is released.

1 S	Facing LOD, RF forward	*One
1	Hold position	Two

2 Q	Continue turning right to face wall, LF a small step to side	Three

3 Q	Close RF to LF. (Now back to back with your partner)	Four

4 S	Turn left to face LOD, LF forward	*One
4	Hold position	Two

5 Q	Continue turning left to face centre, RF a small step to side	Three

6 Q	Close LF to RF. (Now facing partner again)	Four

Repeat these six steps, then resume any hold and continue with the
Basic Movement. ***One**

Two

THE PROMENADE ROCK

Three

Precede with the Cross Basic to the Left turning right into PP as illustrated
opposite. (Facing LOD.) Start position (feet not illustrated). Weight on LF. **Four**

1 S	RF forward still facing LOD	*One
1	Hold position	Two

2 Q	Rock back onto LF (Fallaway Position)	Three

3 Q	Rock forward onto RF (in PP)	Four

4 S	LF forward and across (still in PP), start turning left	*One
4	Hold position	Two

5 Q	Turn left to face partner. RF to the side	Three

6 Q	Close LF to RF	Four

As an alternative, you may dance steps 1–3 three times with alternate feet (starting
with RF the first time) before dancing steps 4–6 thus extending the figure during
two more bars of music. Follow with any other Bossa Nova figure.

THE FACE TO FACE AND BACK TO BACK

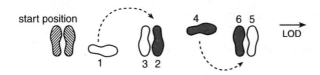

start position

LOD

THE CROSS BASIC TO THE LEFT
(turning right into PP)

LOD

THE PROMENADE ROCK

(also step 6 of
Cross Basic
shown above)

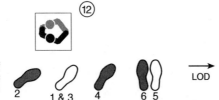

LOD

Perfecting your Bossa Nova technique

Starting

The first beat in each bar is emphasized – but the emphasis varies. It may be subtle if you listen to authentic Bossa Nova music. It will be unmistakable if you listen to Baion music. But, if you listen carefully, you can recognize each first beat – whatever the band plays.

To synchronize your steps with the rhythm, count *one two three four* in time with the music; then step off on the next beat *one*.

Footwork and hip action

Stepping off with a slow step, which is spread over two beats, then following with two quick steps, which seem almost like marking time, gives the Bossa Nova a rather laid-back feel. It has a noticeably lazier hip swing than the Rumba and the Mambo, each of which step off with a quick step.

A slow-motion play back of the slow first step would show the foot sliding across the floor with the ball in contact and the knee slightly bent. As the heel lowers and the knee straightens, the hips swing over this foot, transferring weight to it while the heel of the trailing foot lifts. The ankle and knee action, the hip swing and the weight transfer are the same in quick steps even though the stepping foot may stay in place.

Free arms

During one-hand holds, your free arm should be extended to the side in a gentle curve with the hand held palm down just above the level of your waist. When dancing without hold, each arm should swing rhythmically, as when running, with your hands held in front of your body at the level of your bent elbows.

Partner's roles

The man should choreograph the dance, deciding which figures to dance and their sequence. The woman should follow – even when her partner's decisions surprise her. When dancing without hold she must accept his challenges and follow as quickly as she can.

Experienced dancers find the Bossa Nova pleasurable because of its unusual rhythm and relaxed leg and hip action.

Alternative choreographies

The figures, in the order presented in this chapter, form an excellent routine. A styling suggestion for the Cross Basic is to dance a wider side step on step 1 while swaying away from your supporting foot (if you step with your LF, sway to your right). The wide side step creates an interesting *drag effect* as the foot closes and the sway gives the body a pleasing outline.

a Side Basic.
   Solo Turn to left (woman's right) followed immediately with a Solo Turn to right (woman's left).

b Cross Basic.
   Steps 1–3 of Face to Face and Back to Back.
   Side Basic to right (woman's left).
   Steps 1–3 of Face to Face and Back to Back.
   Side Basic to right (woman's left).

c Cross Basic.
   The Promenade Rock.
   Solo Turn and Side Basic.

d Cross Basic.
   The Promenade Rock.
   Face to Face and Back to Back.

7 | MERENGUE

The *Hispaniola*, the ship in which Jim Hawkins and Long John Silver set sail in search of treasure, took her name from the second largest of the islands in the necklace which encircles the Caribbean Sea. It lies between Cuba and Puerto Rico and has been divided since 1697. The west is Haiti. The larger, eastern part is the Dominican Republic – home to more than seven million people whose national dance, the Merengue (pronounced *merengay*), is exported far and wide by tourists infected by the music while on holiday in this sunny land.

Merengue music is in 2/4 time (two beats to each bar). Its lively tempo (55–60 bars per minute) and emphatic *one-two* rhythm (to which two steps are danced) make it sound like a quick Samba. But it is not. The Merengue has no bounce and its step patterns are simpler. If you can walk, you can Merengue – no matter how small or crowded the dance floor may be!

Hips and steps

All steps are taken ball flat, with a flexed knee which straightens as weight is transferred onto the stepping foot. But the weight transfer occurs later than in the Rumba or the Cha-cha-cha. As a step is taken, the hips remain initially over the *stationary foot* and then, like a pendulum under a poised upper body, they swing away over the stepping foot and weight is transferred.

Basic figures comprise very small forwards, backwards or sideways (side-close) steps which may follow straight or curving paths. These are punctuated by even simpler stepping-in-place (marking time) figures, with the feet almost together, and by rocking movements. The Basic Side Step (on the following pages) which is danced with the man facing the wall and his partner facing the centre, serves as a framework into which other figures are fitted.

Holds

The normal hold position, with the upper body held as still as possible and the arms braced, is the same as the Mambo's. Action is concentrated in the hips and the legs.

Footwork

Footwork to be ball flat.

Figure 7.1   Normal hold position

STEPS	**THE BASIC IN PLACE**	BEATS

Start and finish positions (feet illustrated) facing partner.
Normal hold. Weight on RF. (Facing wall.) — **Two**
(marking time)

1	Lift and replace LF	*One
2	Lift and replace RF	Two
3	Lift and replace LF	*One
4	Lift and replace RF	Two

5–8 Repeat these four steps. You may rotate this figure gradually
to the left or to the right — *One

THE BASIC SIDE STEP

Start and finish positions (feet illustrated) as for the Basic in Place. — **Two**
(sideways to the left)

1	LF a small step to the side	*One
2	Close RF to LF	Two
3	LF a small step to the side	*One
4	Close RF to LF	Two

5–8 Repeat these four steps (rotating gradually to the left if you
wish) then *either* repeat steps 1–8 *or* continue as below. — *One

— **Two**

(sideways to the right)

1	Lift and replace LF	*One
2	RF a small step to the side	Two
3	Close LF to RF	*One
4	RF a small step to the side	Two

5–8 Repeat steps 3 and 4 *twice*.

— *One

THE BASIC SIDE STEP TO FALLAWAY

Start and finish positions (feet illustrated) as for the Basic in Place. — **Two**
1–4 Dance the first four steps of the Basic Side Step.

5	Turn left side away from partner. LF back in fallaway position	*One
6	Transfer weight forward onto RF, in PP	Two
7	Turn right to face partner. LF a small step to the side	*One
8	Close RF to LF. Follow with any Merengue figure	Two

THE BASIC IN PLACE

```
1 ⬤◯ 2
3      4
5      6
7 ⬤◯ 8
```

THE BASIC SIDE STEP

LOD ⟵

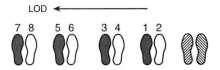

against LOD ⟶

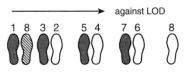

⟵ LOD

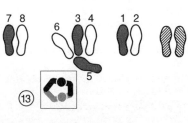

STEPS	**THE PROMENADE FLICK**	BEATS

Start and finish positions (feet illustrated) as for the Basic in Place.

1–4 Dance the first four steps of the Basic Side Step turning left on step four into PP (facing LOD) — **Two**

5 LF forward in PP. Flick RF back keeping knees together — ***One**

6 RF forward and across, still in PP — **Two**

7 Turning right to face partner, LF a small step to the side — ***One**

8 Close RF to LF — **Two**

Follow with any Merengue figure.

As an alternative dance steps 1–4 *once*, then steps 5 and 6 *three times*, then steps 7 and 8 *once*, (twelve steps in all) then dance the Basic in Place or the Basic Side Step to complete sixteen steps. — ***One**

— **Two**

— ***One**

THE SEPARATION

— **Two**

Start and finish positions (feet illustrated) as for the Basic in Place.

1 LF a very small step back, easing partner away — ***One**

2 RF a very small step back, still easing partner away — **Two**

3–8 Repeat steps 1 and 2 three times while extending your left arm and sliding your RH along your partner's left arm to finish in double hold — ***One** **Two**

9 LF a very small step forward, slowly drawing partner closer — ***One**

10 RF a very small step forward, still drawing partner closer — **Two**

11–16 Repeat steps 9 and 10 *three times* while drawing your partner closer to finish in normal hold. — ***One**

Follow with another separation *or* with the Basic Side Step *or* with the Separation with Arm Circle (below). — **Two**

— ***One**

THE SEPARATION WITH ARM CIRCLE

— **Two**

Start and finish positions (feet not illustrated) as for the Basic in Place.

1–16 Dance the Separation but change hands to palm to palm contact while dancing steps 9–12, then raise your hands above your heads and begin to circle them outwards while dancing steps 13–16 — ***One** **Two**

17–24 Dance four backward walks followed by four forward walks while circling your hands outwards, downwards and upwards, resuming normal hold for the Basic Side Step — ***One** **Two**

THE PROMENADE FLICK

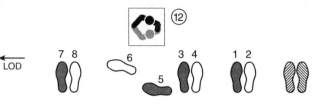

THE SEPARATION

(facing wall)

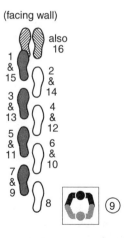

THE SEPARATION
WITH ARM CIRCLE

1-16 the first sixteen
steps as opposite

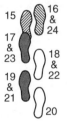

STEPS ## THE COPY-CAT TURNS

BEATS

Start positions (feet not illustrated) double hold, weight on
RF (facing wall) having danced steps 1–8 of the Separation.

Two

1–8 Starting with the LF, dance the Basic in Place and, while holding
your partner's hands close together, circle your joined hands
anti-clockwise above your partner's head so that she makes
a complete turn to her left before you lower your hands to
waist level on step 8. Your wrists are now crossed with your
right wrists uppermost.

*One

Two

*One

Two

9–16 As you continue dancing the Basic in Place, raise your joined
hands again above your heads then, while your partner stays
in place, make a complete turn to your right under raised
hands. Finish facing your partner with lowered hands and
uncrossed wrists.

*One

Two

*One

Follow with another Copy-Cat Turn or with the Separation
ending in normal hold before dancing any other Merengue figure.

Two

THE WINDMILL

*One

Start and finish position (feet not illustrated) as for the Copy-Cat Turns.

Two

1–8 Starting with your LF, dance tiny forward steps but turn under
raised hands – you to your left and your partner to her right.
Finish as on step 16 of the Copy-Cat Turns.

*One

These eight steps may be repeated.

Two

THE SIDE WALK

*One

Start position (feet illustrated) as for the Basic in Place.

Two

1–4 Dance four steps of the Basic Side Step

5	LF a small step to the side	*One
6	Close RF to LF	and
7	LF a small step to the side	Two
8	Close RF to LF	and
9	LF a *long* step to the side	*One
10	Close RF to LF.	Two

Follow with the Basic in Place or with any other Merengue figure.

THE COPY-CAT TURNS

Basic in Place while partner turns

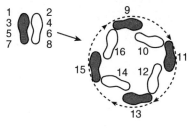

THE WINDMILL

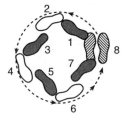

THE SIDE WALK

LOD ←

start position having danced
1-4 of the Basic Side Step

STEPS	**THE BASIC IN PLACE**	BEATS

Start and finish positions (feet illustrated) facing partner.

Normal hold. Weight on LF. (Facing centre.)   **Two**

(marking time)

1	Lift and replace RF	*One
2	Lift and replace LF	Two
3	Lift and replace RF	*One
4	Lift and replace LF	Two

5–8 Repeat these four steps. You may rotate this figure gradually to the left or to the right.   *One

THE BASIC SIDE STEP

Start and finish positions (feet illustrated) as for the Basic in Place.   **Two**

(sideways to the right)

1	RF a small step to the side	*One
2	Close LF to RF	Two
3	RF a small step to the side	*One
4	Close LF to RF	Two

5–8 Repeat these four steps (rotating gradually to the left if you wish) then *either* repeat steps 1–8 *or* continue as below.   *One

                                                                         Two

(sideways to the left)

1	Lift and replace RF	*One
2	LF a small step to the side	Two
3	Close RF to LF	*One
4	LF a small step to the side	Two

5–8 Repeat steps 3 and 4 *twice*.

                                                                         *One

THE BASIC SIDE STEP TO FALLAWAY

Start and finish positions (feet illustrated) as for the Basic in Place.   **Two**

1–4 Dance the first four steps of the Basic Side Step.

5	Turn right side away from partner. RF back in fallaway position	*One
6	Transfer weight forward onto LF, in PP	Two
7	Turn left to face partner. RF a small step to the side	*One
8	Close LF to RF. Follow with any Merengue figure	Two

THE BASIC IN PLACE

```
2  ◖◗  1
4      3
6      5
8      7
```

THE BASIC SIDE STEP

⟶ LOD

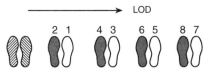

against LOD ⟵

```
8    6 7    4 5    2 3  8 1
◖    ◖◗    ◖◗    ◖◗  ◖◗
```

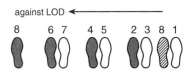

⟶
LOD

STEPS	**THE PROMENADE FLICK**	BEATS

Start and finish positions (feet illustrated) as for the Basic in Place.

1–4	Dance the first four steps of the Basic Side Step turning right on step four into PP (facing LOD)	Two
5	RF forward in PP. Flick LF back keeping knees together	*One
6	LF forward and across, still in PP	Two
7	Turning left to face partner, RF a small step to the side	*One
8	Close LF to RF	Two

Follow with any Merengue figure.

As an alternative dance steps 1–4 *once*, then steps 5 and 6 *three times*, then steps 7 and 8 *once*, (twelve steps in all) then dance the Basic in Place or the Basic Side Step to complete sixteen steps.

*One

Two

*One

THE SEPARATION

Two

Start and finish positions (feet illustrated) as for the Basic in Place.

1	RF a very small step back, moving away from partner	*One
2	LF a very small step back, still moving away from partner	Two
3–8	Repeat steps 1 and 2 three times while extending your arms as you both continue to move away from each other to finish in double hold	*One Two
9	RF a very small step forward, slowly moving towards partner	*One
10	LF a very small step forward, still moving towards partner	Two
11–16	Repeat steps 9 and 10 *three times* while moving closer to each other to finish in normal hold.	*One

Follow with another separation *or* with the Basic Side Step *or* with the Separation with Arm Circle (below).

Two

*One

THE SEPARATION WITH ARM CIRCLE

Two

Start and finish position (feet not illustrated) as for the Basic in Place.

1–16	Dance the Separation but change hands to palm to palm contact while dancing steps 9–12, then raise your hands above your heads and begin to circle them outwards while dancing steps 13–16	*One Two
17–24	Dance four backward walks followed by four forward walks while circling your hands outwards, downwards and upwards, resuming normal hold for the Basic Side Step	*One Two

THE PROMENADE FLICK

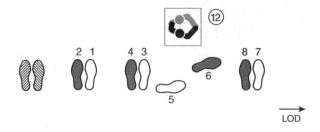

LOD

THE SEPARATION

(facing centre)

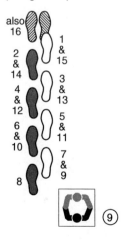

THE SEPARATION WITH ARM CIRCLE

1-16 the first sixteen steps as opposite

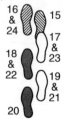

STEPS **THE COPY-CAT TURNS** BEATS

Start positions (feet not illustrated) double hold, weight on
LF (facing centre) having danced steps 1–8 of the Separation. | Two

1–8 Starting with the RF, dance the Basic in Place and, while your | *One
joined hands are held close together and raised above your
head, leading you to make a complete turn to your left | Two
before your hands are lowered to waist level on step 8.
Your wrists are now crossed with your right wrists | *One
uppermost.

| Two

9–16 As you continue dancing the Basic in Place, your joined hands | *One
are raised again above your partner's head as he makes a
complete turn to his right while you stay in place to finish, | Two
facing each other once more with lowered hands and
uncrossed wrists. | *One

Follow with another Copy-Cat Turn or with the Separation ending in
normal hold before dancing any other Merengue figure. | Two

| *One

THE WINDMILL

Start and finish position (feet not illustrated) as for the | Two
Copy-Cat Turns.

1–8 Starting with your RF, dance tiny forward steps but turn under | *One
raised hands – you to your right and your partner to his left.
Finish as on step 16 of the Copy-Cat Turns. | Two

These eight steps may be repeated.

| *One

THE SIDE WALK

Start position (feet illustrated) as for the Basic in Place. | Two

1–4 Dance four steps of the Basic Side Step.

5	RF a small step to the side	*One
6	Close LF to RF	and
7	RF a small step to the side	Two
8	Close LF to RF	and
9	RF a *long* step to the side	*One
10	Close LF to RF.	Two

Follow with the Basic in Place or with any other Merengue figure.

THE COPY-CAT TURNS

Basic in Place while partner turns

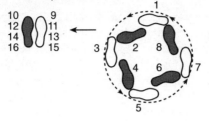

THE WINDMILL

THE SIDE WALK

start position having danced
1-4 of the Basic Side Step

LOD

Perfecting your Merengue technique

Starting

While the Merengue's emphatic beat makes starting simple, some beats are better than others. It is worthwhile listening to the wind and string instruments, or to the vocalist, because you will find that the tune fits into a four-bar period – the same period that the eight-step figures require – so try to step off on a first beat which synchronizes with the melody. Some dancers find that it helps to count *one-two-three-four* over the previous two bars before stepping off.

Footwork and the Merengue action

On beat one, the inside edge of the ball of the *stepping foot* (beneath a slightly flexed knee) makes contact with the floor while the hips remain over the stationary *supporting foot*.

On beat two the feet change roles. As its heel lowers and knee straightens, the stepping foot takes the weight and becomes the supporting foot when the hips swing over it. Meanwhile the inside edge of the ball of the other, unweighted foot is placed in a new position beneath a flexed knee.

You may find it helps to count *ah-one ah-two* – swinging your hips over the heel that has just been lowered on the *ahs* before taking each step.

The Merengue hip-swinging action is, of course, continuous. You don't have time to consider each tiny facet. Keep your upper body as still as possible while letting your hips and legs move in time with the catchy music.

Partner's roles

Merengue is infectious and lighthearted – even playful – and, as you gain confidence, it invites you to improvise. Punctuate the easy walking steps with a turn to match the music's mood; dance it under one raised arm or under two. Turn simultaneously with your partner or turn alternately. Improvising is easy providing the man decides and gently leads his partner before she anticipates another figure.

Alternative choreographies

a The Basic in Place.
The Basic Side Step to
  Fallaway.
1–4 Basic Side Step.
1–4 Basic in Place.

b The Basic Side Step.
The Basic Side Step to
  Right (woman's left).
4 Back Walks (woman
  forward).
4 Forward Walks (woman
  back).
4 Back Walks (woman
  forward).
4 Forward Walks (woman
  back).
The Promenade Flick.

c The Basic Side Step.
The Separation into The
  Copy-Cat Turns.

d The Basic Side Step.
The Separation with Arm
  Circles.
The Promenade Flick.
The Side Walk.

e The Basic in Place.
The Separation into The
  Windmill (twice).
1–2 Basic Side Step.
2 Hip Rocks (feet in place).
1–2 Basic Side Step.
2 Hip Rocks (feet in place).

f The Basic in Place (raising
  hands above heads).
The Basic in Place while
  turning woman to her
  right then to her left.
The Promenade Flick
  (Alternative.)

8 | SALSA

Many artists and musicians fled from Cuba, following Fidel Castro's 1958 coup, and settled in New York. The New Yorkers soon became aware of unfamiliar but intriguing rhythms played on bongo drums and maracas that the Cubans had brought with them. For the exiles there was also a surprise in store. They were bewitched by the sound of jazz played on trumpets and trombones in American and Puerto Rican bands.

A liaison was inevitable. The mainlanders fell for the rhythm and the percussion while the islanders were seduced by the brass. A new sound was born that was christened *Salsa*, which means *sauce*, and may be an abbreviated form of the Spanish exhortation *Echale salista!*, meaning *Spice it up!*

The Salsa belongs to the Cha-cha-cha–Rumba–Mambo rhythmic family, and couples dancing it do not travel around the floor but rotate and turn in their own space – which may be small if the floor is crowded. Because the dance is still evolving, regional variations will be encountered if you travel in South America and the Caribbean Islands, in the US, or in Britain, where there are fifty or more Salsa dance clubs.

Salsa music is in 4/4 time (four beats to each bar) and may vary in tempo from 40 to 52 bars per minute. Do not despair if it sounds busy and disorganized. Most people have to listen carefully at first – to separate the underlying beat from the rattle of maracas – but, when you have learned the trick, it is hard to ignore the rhythm.

The basic steps are easy. Three little marching steps (often danced on the spot) are followed by a *tap* (made with the ball of your big toe) on beat four. Later you will learn to dance a *flick* (with your lower leg) or a *point* (downwards with a straight knee and your foot held off the floor) or even to *hold* (the position of the third step) instead of dancing a tap. Dancing a *hold* converts the timing from *quick-quick-quick-quick* to *quick-quick-slow*. Practise the following solo exercise before learning the Side Basic on the next page.

Dance three little marching steps on the spot followed by a tap, keeping in time with the music. When this feels completely natural, practise rotating the steps gently to the right.

Holds

There are two normal holds – close contact and double hold. Partners stand tall in each of them, with their upper bodies poised, so that their hips can move freely.

In close contact, the woman stands with her partner's right foot between her toes and is held in contact by his right hand behind her waist. She rests her left hand where she pleases – on his upper arm, on his shoulder, or on the back of his neck. Their joined hands are held lightly at about his eye level.

In double hold, partners stand apart with hands held palm to palm (fingers pointing upwards) just below the man's shoulder height. Arms are lightly braced and elbows are held away from their bodies.

Footwork

Footwork to be ball flat unless instructed otherwise.

Figure 8.1 Close contact and double hold positions

STEPS	**THE SIDE BASIC**	BEATS

Start position (feet not illustrated). Normal or double hold.
Feet together. Weight on RF.

Four

1	LF a small step to the side	*One
2	Close RF to LF	Two
3	LF a small step to the side	Three
4	Tap inside edge of ball of RF close to LF	Four
5	RF a small step to the side	*One
6	Close LF to RF	Two
7	RF a small step to the side	Three
8	Tap inside edge of ball of LF close to RF	Four

Repeat as you wish. You may rotate the figure gently to the right. Follow
with any other figure in this chapter.

*One

Two

Three

THE BACK BASIC

Start position (feet not illustrated). Normal or double hold.
Feet together. Weight on RF.

Four

1	LF a small step back. (Your partner also steps back)	*One
2	Transfer weight forward onto RF	Two
3	Close LF to RF. (You both return to your start position)	Three
4	Tap inside edge of ball of RF close to LF	Four
5	RF a small step back. (Your partner also steps back)	*One
6	Transfer weight forward onto LF	Two
7	Close RF to LF. (You both return to your start position)	Three
8	Tap the inside edge of the ball of LF close to RF	Four

Repeat as you wish. This is an important linking figure. The first or the
second half may form part of another figure.
Follow with any other figure in this chapter.

THE SIDE BASIC

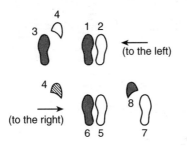

THE BACK BASIC

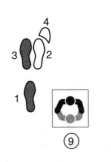
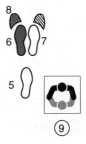

STEPS	**THE CROSS BASIC**	BEATS

Start position (feet not illustrated). Normal or double hold.
Feet together. Weight on RF.

Four

(to the left)

1	LF back and slightly to the left. (Partner also steps back)	*One
2	RF a small step across and in front of LF	Two
3	Close LF *almost* to RF	Three
4	Tap inside edge of ball of RF close to LF	Four

--------------(to the right)--------------

5	RF back and slightly to the right. (Partner also steps back)	*One
6	LF a small step across in front of RF	Two
7	Close RF *almost* to LF	Three
8	Tap inside edge of ball of LF close to RF	Four

Repeat as you wish. Do not turn your upper body when you step across on steps 3 and 6. Partners should keep their shoulders parallel.
Follow with any other figure in this chapter.

*One

Two

	THE ROCK BASIC (Cucarachas)	**Three**

Start position (feet not illustrated). Normal or double hold.
Feet together. Weight on RF.

Four

(to the left)

1	LF to the side with pressure, leaving RF in place	*One
2	Transfer weight sideways onto RF	Two
3	Close LF to RF	Three
4	Tap inside edge of ball of RF close to LF	Four

--------------(to the right)--------------

5	RF to the side with pressure, leaving LF in place	*One
6	Transfer weight sideways onto LF	Two
7	Close RF to LF	Three
8	Tap the inside edge of the ball of LF close to RF	Four

Repeat as you wish. Follow with any other figure in this chapter.

THE CROSS BASIC

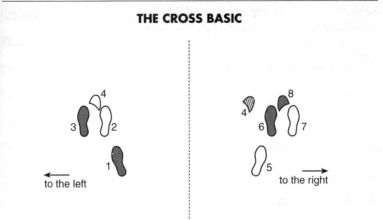

to the left

to the right

THE ROCK BASIC (Cucarachas)

to the left

to the right

STEPS	**THE OPENING OUT BASIC**	BEATS

Start position (feet not illustrated). Normal or double hold.
Feet together. Weight on RF. Lead partner to turn to her right. **Four**
Release LH.

1	Turn a quarter to the left into RSP. LF to the side	*One
2	Transfer weight onto RF. Start turning right	Two
3	Close LF to RF. Now facing partner. Regain DH	Three
4	Tap inside edge of ball of RF close to LF	Four

----------------Lead partner to turn to her left. Release RH----------------

5	Turn a quarter to the right into LSP. RF to the side	*One
6	Transfer weight onto LF. Start turning left	Two
7	Close RF to LF. Now facing partner. Regain DH	Three
8	Tap inside edge of ball of LF close to RF	Four

Repeat as you wish. On steps 1 and 5 you may step back instead of sideways
as in the Hand to Hand of the Rumba. On steps 1 and 5 you may hold your   ***One**
partner around her waist instead of holding her hand. Follow with any other
figure in this chapter.

     Two

     Three

THE BACK BASIC INTO OPENING OUT

Start position (feet not illustrated). Normal or double hold.   **Four**
Feet together. Weight on RF.

1	LF a small step back. (Your partner also steps back)	*One
2	Transfer weight forward onto RF	Two
3	Close LF to RF. (You both return to your start position)	Three
4	Tap inside edge of ball of RF close to LF	Four

----------------Lead partner to turn to her left. Release RH----------------

5	Turn a quarter to the right into LSP. RF to the side	*One
6	Transfer weight onto LF. Start turning left	Two
7	Close RF to LF. Now facing partner. Regain DH	Three
8	Tap inside edge of ball of LF close to RF	Four

Either repeat (as you wish) *or* repeat it after dancing the next figure
(The Woman's Underarm Turn to Left). Follow with any other figure in
this chapter.

THE OPENING OUT BASIC

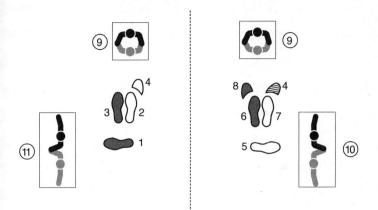

THE BACK BASIC INTO OPENING OUT

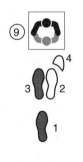
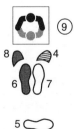

STEPS	**THE WOMAN'S UNDERARM TURN TO THE LEFT** **(with Back Basic)**	BEATS
	Start position (feet not illustrated). Normal or double hold. Feet together. Weight on RF. (Facing centre.)	**Four**
1	LF a small step back (partner also steps back). Release RH. (Raise LH to lead partner to turn to her left.)	*One
2	RF forward and across LF while turning right	Two
3	After a quarter turn, close LF almost to RF still turning partner	Three
4	Tap inside edge of ball of RF close to LF. Regain DH. (Facing LOD)	Four
5	RF a small step back. (Your partner also steps back)	*One
6	Transfer weight forward onto LF	Two
7	Close RF to LF. (You both return to your start position)	Three
8	Tap the inside edge of the ball of LF close to RF	Four
	Either repeat (as you wish) *or* repeat it after dancing the previous figure (the Back Basic into Opening Out). Follow with any other figure in this chapter.	*One
		Two
		Three

THE ALTERNATE TURNS

	Start position (feet not illustrated). Normal or double hold. Feet together. Weight on RF. (Facing wall.)	Four
1	LF a small step back. (Your partner also steps back)	*One
2	Transfer weight forward onto RF. Start turning right. Raise LH. (Release RH)	Two
3	While turning right under your raised hand, close LF to RF	Three
4	Tap inside edge of ball of RF close to LF. Now backing partner. (Facing centre)	Four
5	RF a turning step close to LF, still turning right	*One
6	LF a turning step close to RF, still turning	Two
7	RF a turning step close to LF, still turning right	Three
8	Tap inside edge of ball of LF close to RF. (Now facing wall)	Four

9–16 Keep joined hands raised leading your partner to dance a full
turn to her left while you dance the eight steps of your Back
Basic. Follow with any Salsa figure over two more bars of music.

THE WOMAN'S UNDERARM TURN TO THE LEFT
(with Back Basic)

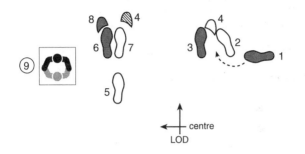

THE ALTERNATE TURNS

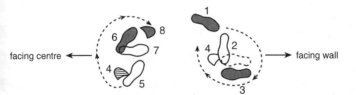

Steps 9 - 16 dance the Back Basic while your partner turns

STEPS	**THE SIDE BASIC**	BEATS

Start position (feet not illustrated). Normal or double hold.
Feet together. Weight on LF. **Four**

1	RF a small step to the side	*One
2	Close LF to RF	Two
3	RF a small step to the side	Three
4	Tap inside edge of ball of LF close to RF	Four
5	LF a small step to the side	*One
6	Close RF to LF	Two
7	LF a small step to the side	Three
8	Tap inside edge of ball of RF close to LF	Four

Repeat as you wish. This figure may be rotated gently to the right. Follow with
any other figure in this chapter. ***One**

Two

Three

THE BACK BASIC

Four

Start position (feet not illustrated). Normal or double hold.
Feet together. Weight on LF.

1	RF a small step back. (Your partner also steps back)	*One
2	Transfer weight forwards onto LF	Two
3	Close RF to LF. (You both return to your start position)	Three
4	Tap inside edge of ball of LF close to RF	Four
5	LF a small step back. (Your partner also steps back)	*One
6	Transfer weight forward onto RF	Two
7	Close LF to RF. (You both return to your start position)	Three
8	Tap the inside edge of the ball of RF close to LF	Four

Repeat as you wish. This is an important linking figure. The first or the second half
may form part of another figure.
Follow with any other figure in this chapter.

THE SIDE BASIC

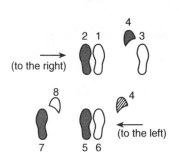

THE BACK BASIC

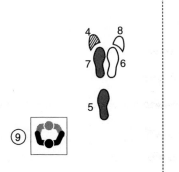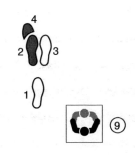

STEPS	**THE CROSS BASIC**	BEATS
	Start position (feet not illustrated). Normal or double hold.	
	Feet together. Weight on LF.	Four
	(to the right)	
1	RF back and slightly to the right. (Partner also steps back)	*One
2	LF a small step across and in front of RF	Two
3	Close RF *almost* to LF	Three
4	Tap inside edge of ball of LF close to RF	Four
	----------------(to the left)--	
5	LF back and slightly to the left. (Partner also steps back)	*One
6	RF a small step across in front of LF	Two
7	Close LF *almost* to RF	Three
8	Tap inside edge of ball of RF close to LF	Four
	Repeat as you wish. Do not turn your upper body when you step across on steps 3 and 6. Partners should keep their shoulders parallel.	*One
	Follow with any other figure in this chapter.	
		Two

STEPS	**THE ROCK BASIC (Cucarachas)**	BEATS
		Three
	Start position (feet not illustrated). Normal or double hold.	
	Feet together. Weight on LF.	Four
	(to the left)	
1	RF to the side with pressure, leaving LF in place	*One
2	Transfer weight sideways onto LF	Two
3	Close RF to LF	Three
4	Tap inside edge of ball of LF close to RF	Four
	----------------(to the left)--	
5	LF to the side with pressure, leaving RF in place	*One
6	Transfer weight sideways onto RF	Two
7	Close LF to RF	Three
8	Tap the inside edge of the ball of RF close to LF	Four
	Repeat as you wish. Follow with any other figure in this chapter.	

THE CROSS BASIC

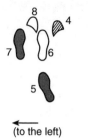

(to the left)

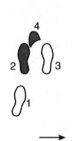

(to the right)

THE ROCK BASIC (Cucarachas)

to the left

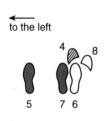

to the right

STEPS	**THE OPENING OUT BASIC**	BEATS
	Start position (feet not illustrated). Normal or double hold.	
	Feet together. Weight on LF. Your partner will lead you to turn right and release your RH.	**Four**
1	Turn a quarter to the right into LSP. RF to the side	***One**
2	Transfer weight onto LF. Start turning left	**Two**
3	Close RF to LF. Now facing partner. Regain DH	**Three**
4	Tap inside edge of ball of LF close to RF	**Four**
	--------Your partner will lead you to turn left and release LH------------------------------------	
5	Turn a quarter to the left into RSP. LF to the side	***One**
6	Transfer weight onto RF. Start turning right	**Two**
7	Close LF to RF. Now facing partner. Regain DH	**Three**
8	Tap inside edge of ball of RF close to LF	**Four**
	Repeat as you wish. On steps 1 and 5 you may step back instead of sideways as in the Hand to Hand of the Rumba. On steps 1 and 5 your partner may place his arm around your waist instead of holding your hand. If so, place your hand across his shoulder blades. Follow with any other figure in this chapter.	***One**
		Two
		Three

THE BACK BASIC INTO OPENING OUT

	Start position (feet not illustrated). Normal or double hold.	**Four**
	Feet together. Weight on LF.	
1	RF a small step back. (Your partner also steps back)	***One**
2	Transfer weight forward onto LF	**Two**
3	Close RF to LF. (You both return to your start position)	**Three**
4	Tap inside edge of ball of LF close to RF	**Four**
	--------Your partner will lead you to turn left and release your LH --------------------------------	
5	Turn a quarter to the left into RSP. LF to the side	***One**
6	Transfer weight onto RF. Start turning right	**Two**
7	Close LF to RF. Now facing partner. Regain DH	**Three**
8	Tap inside edge of ball of RF close to LF	**Four**

Either repeat (as you wish) *or* repeat it after dancing the next figure
(The Woman's Underarm Turn to the Left). Follow with any other figure in
this chapter.

THE OPENING OUT BASIC

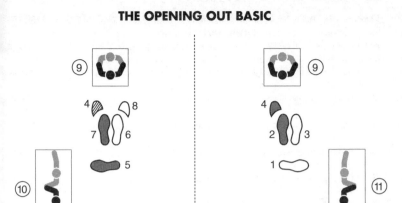

THE BACK BASIC INTO OPENING OUT

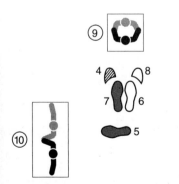

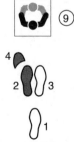

STEPS	**THE WOMAN'S UNDERARM TURN TO THE LEFT**	BEATS
	(with Back Basic)	

Precede with the Back Basic. Start position (feet not illustrated).   **Four**
Normal or double hold. Feet together. Weight on LF. (Facing wall.)

1	RF a small step back (partner also steps back)	*One
	(Your RH is raised to lead you to turn left. LH is released)	
2	Turn a quarter left to face LOD. LF a small step forward	Two
3	On LF swivel a half turn to the left. Close RF almost to LF	Three
	(Now facing against LOD.)	
4	Tap inside edge of ball of LF close to RF. Regain DH	Four
5	LF a small step back. (Your partner also steps back)	*One
6	Transfer weight forward onto RF	Two
7	Close LF to RF. (You both return to your start position)	Three
8	Tap the inside edge of the ball of RF close to LF	Four

Either repeat (as your partner wishes) *or* repeat it after dancing the previous
figure. Follow with any other figure in this chapter.   *One

THE ALTERNATE TURNS   Two

Start position (feet not illustrated). Normal or double hold. Weight on LF.
(Facing centre.)   Three

1–8	LH is released, RH is raised. Step RF back into the Back Basic	Four
	as your partner turns right under joined hands.	
9	RF a step in place beside LF. Start turning left under raised hands	*One
10	LF a turning step close to RF, still turning left	Two
11	RF a turning step close to LF, still turning	Three
12	Tap inside edge of ball of LF close to RF. Now backing partner.	Four
	(Facing wall)	
13	LF a step in place beside RF. Still turning left under raised hands	*One
14	RF a turning step close to LF, still turning	Two
15	LF a turning step close to RF, still turning	Three
16	Tap inside edge of ball of RF close to LF. Now facing partner.	Four
	(Facing centre again)	

These sixteen steps are danced over four bars of music. The figure may be danced
turning right (man left). Follow with any other figure in this chapter.

THE WOMAN'S UNDERARM TURN TO THE LEFT
(with Back Basic)

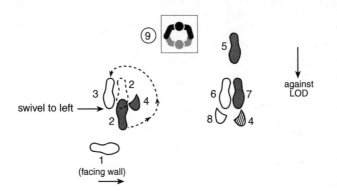

swivel to left ➝

against
LOD

1
(facing wall)
➝

THE ALTERNATE TURNS

Steps 1 - 8 dance the Back Basic while your partner turns

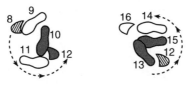

centre ◄——— ——➤ wall

Perfecting your Salsa technique

Starting

Count yourself in over a couple of bars, then step off on beat one as shown on the preceding pages. Some people like to dance the *tap* on beat one instead of on the previous beat four. This is fine – but keep your partner in the picture.

Footwork and basic action

Nearly all steps are danced ball flat. Taps are danced with pressure.

The Salsa seems busy because its tempo is quick and because, usually, some movement is danced on each beat. Small quick steps, well cushioned by supple ankles and knees, do impart a slight but distinctive Salsa hip swing, but there is not time for the pronounced hip sway of the Rumba and the Cha-cha-cha.

Arms and hands

Besides giving the dance its distinctive *Salsa* look, the double hold – with braced elbows held wide – makes it easy to lead the turns and to lift your joined hands so that they pass over your heads while you are dancing them. To be out of the way, during turns, free arms should be held close to your body, but elbows should be bent and relaxed to make resuming hold easy.

Partner's roles

The man must lead firmly and gently and the woman must respond readily. There are so many possible choreography variations that it is helpful to plan a short routine before enjoying yourselves on the dance floor.

Alternative choreographies

Try to group figures together in four-bar sequences to mirror the phrasing of the music.

a The Side Basic (rotating).
The Rock Basic.
The Back Basic.
The Cross Basic.

b The Basic in Place
(rotating).
The Rock Basic.
The Opening Out Basic.
The Side Basic.

c The Back Basic into
Opening Out (twice).
The Rock Basic.
The Woman's Underarm
Turn to the Left (with
Back Basic) (twice).
The Back Basic.

d The Back Basic into
Opening Out.
The Woman's Underarm
Turn to the Left (with
Back Basic).
Repeat these two figures
alternately.
The Alternate Turns.

9 | JIVE

The Jive does not progress around the dance floor, but it is a fine party dance because its figures are danced in a small space and may be started facing any direction – the alignment suggestions on the following figure pages are given solely as an aid to learning.

The dance is a scrap of American history: in the Second World War it reminded GIs of home and they left it behind them in every country through which they passed. Its music, in 4/4 time (four beats to each bar) has a tempo of 40–46 bars per minute.

As a juvenile, named the Jitterbug, the Jive was so much given to hazardous lifts and jumps that it was banished from many American dance halls. It survived, of course, as the Lindy, the West Coast Swing, the American Swing and the still popular Rock 'n' Roll and, in all these guises, retained its distinctive, carefree character. While his feet beat out the rhythm, the man leads his partner to turn underarm to right and left, to spin and to pass behind his back.

Each of the following figures has eight steps which are squeezed into six beats (1½ bars) of music. Each figure has two rock-type steps followed by two consecutive three-step chassés. The second step of each chassé is danced between beats and is marked '*a*' in the right, beat-side margin of the step instruction pages. Read down the beat margin of the Fallaway Rock and you will see – *one-two-three-a-four-one-a-two* – which is probably what you will hear your teacher count during each eight-step figure while you dance it. But, if you read further down, you will see two beats (*three-four*) with no steps because the title of the next figure is in the way. When you are dancing, the music goes on and so do you, taking the first step of the next figure on beat *three* of the same bar.

Dancing the Jive is all about dancing its chassés. Each chassé's three tiny steps move in the same general direction – forwards, backwards, sideways or in a curve – and, because the feet never quite close, the following foot never quite catches up with the leading foot. The *beat value* of each chassé step is – first ³/₄, second *a*) ¹/₄, third *1* – but the feeling is quick, light and rhythmical and you won't have time to check this.

Practise the sideways chassés in the Fallaway Rock until you become accustomed to the quick changes of weight and can respond to the rhythm without thinking. Then practise the whole figure before moving on to the Fallaway Throwaway and the Link Rock. These three figures, in this sequence, make a good starter routine; master them before attempting any more.

Holds

The normal hold is looser than in other Latin dances. The man places his right hand just below his partner's left shoulder blade and holds her right hand in his left, a little above waist level, while keeping both arms relaxed. She rests her left arm on his right arm. One-hand hold (the man's right holding the woman's left) is used more frequently than normal hold, and handshake hold (the man's right holding the woman's right) is used quite often.

Footwork

Footwork to be ball flat unless instructed otherwise.

Figure 9.1   Normal hold position

STEPS	**THE FALLAWAY ROCK**	BEATS

Start position (feet not illustrated). Normal hold. Weight on RF.
(Facing wall.)   **Four**

1	Turn left side away from partner. LF back in fallaway position. (Almost facing LOD)	*One
2	Replace weight onto RF, in PP. Start turning right	Two

3	LF a small step to the side, while turning right to face partner	Three
4	Close RF halfway to LF	a
5	LF a small step to the side	Four

6	RF a small step to the side	*One
7	Close LF halfway to RF	a
8	RF a small step to the side	Two

Either repeat these steps *or* follow with the Fallaway Throwaway.

Three

THE FALLAWAY THROWAWAY

Start position (feet not illustrated). Normal hold. Weight on RF.   **Four**
(Facing wall.)

1	Turn left side away from partner. LF back in fallaway position. (Almost facing LOD)	*One
2	Replace weight onto RF, in PP. Start turning partner towards you	Two

3	LF diagonally forward. Start turning left. Partner now facing you	Three
4	Close RF a short way to LF, while turning left to face LOD	a
5	LF a very small step to the side while swaying to left. (Lower LH slightly)	Four
6	RF a small step forward down LOD while recovering sway.	*One
7	Close LF, on ball, halfway to RF. Release RH	a
8	RF a small step forward, now in open facing position	Two

Lead your partner to dance a chassé backwards as you dance a chassé forwards on steps 6, 7 and 8.
Follow with the Link Rock (overleaf).

THE FALLAWAY ROCK

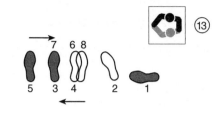

THE FALLAWAY THROWAWAY

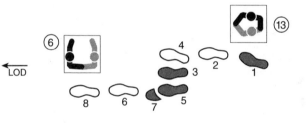

STEPS	**THE LINK ROCK**	BEATS

Start in open facing position (feet not illustrated). RF forward. Weight on RF. (Facing LOD.)

Four

1	LF back	*One

2	Replace weight onto RF	Two

3	LF a very small step forward. Start drawing partner towards you	Three
4	Close RF, on ball, a short way to LF	a
5	LF a very small step forward. Resume normal hold	Four

6	RF a small step to the side	*One
7	Close LF halfway to RF	a
8	RF a small step to the side	Two

Follow with the Fallaway Rock, the Fallaway Throwaway, the Change of Places Right to Left or the Walks in Promenade.

Three

THE CHANGE OF HANDS BEHIND BACK

Start in open facing position (feet not illustrated). RF forward. Weight on RF. (Facing wall.)

Four

1	LF back	*One

2	Replace weight onto RF	Two
	(With LH begin leading your partner towards your right side)	
3	LF forward. Begin turning left so your partner can pass on your right	Three
4	Close RF halfway to LF, still turning	a
5	LF forward, still turning. Take your partner's RH in your RH	Four
	(Then she passes your right side. Change hands behind your back)	
6	Complete a half turn to the left (to face centre). RF back on ball	*One
7	Draw LF back towards RF (moving away from each other)	a
8	RF back to finish in open facing position	Two

Either repeat these eight steps *or* dance the Link Rock or the Change of Places Left to Right.

Three

Four

*One

Two

THE KICK BALL CHANGE

This 'figure', which can be danced in open facing or promenade position, is an alternative way of dancing the first *two beats* of some figures by squeezing in *three steps* instead of two. The rhythm is the same as in the chassés but the steps and action are quite different.

Three

Four

1	Flick LF forward, from the knee, just clear of the floor	*One
2	LF, on ball, a small step back just behind RF	a
3	Replace weight onto RF	Two

THE LINK ROCK

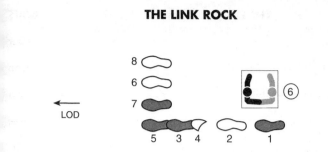

THE CHANGE OF HANDS BEHIND BACK

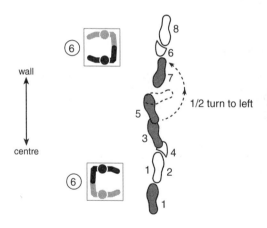

THE KICK BALL CHANGE

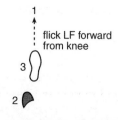

STEPS **THE CHANGE OF PLACES RIGHT TO LEFT**   BEATS

Start position (feet not illustrated). Normal hold. Weight on RF.
(Facing wall.)   **Four**

1	Turn left side away from partner. LF back in fallaway position	***One**
2	Replace weight onto RF, in PP. Start turning right (partner to left)	**Two**
3	LF a small step to the side, while turning to face partner	**Three**
4	Close RF halfway to LF	**a**
5	Start turning left. LF a small step to the side. Raise LH	**Four**
	(Then, with RH, turn partner underarm to her right. Release RH)	
6	RF a small step forward (now facing LOD). Lower joined hands	***One**
7	Close LF, on ball, halfway to RF. Partner has completed turn	**a**
8	RF a small step forward to finish in open facing position	**Two**

Follow with the Link Rock, the Change of Places Left to Right,
the Change of Hands Behind Back or the American Spin.   **Three**

THE CHANGE OF PLACES LEFT TO RIGHT

Start in open facing position (feet not illustrated). RF forward. Weight on RF.   **Four**
(Facing LOD.)

1	LF back	***One**
2	Replace weight onto RF	**Two**
	(Raise LH to lead partner across you to begin turning left)	
3	LF a very small step to the side while turning right (partner turns left)	**Three**
4	Close RF part way to LF. Now facing wall (partner still turning)	**a**
5	Step LF almost in place. Partner's back is now towards you	**Four**
	(Lower LH to lead partner to complete her turn)	
6	RF forward and lead partner (now facing you) to step back	***One**
7	Close LF, on ball, halfway to RF. Partner still moving back	**a**
8	RF a small step forward into open facing position	**Two**

Follow with the Link Rock, the Change of Hands Behind Back or the American
Spin (overleaf).

THE CHANGE OF PLACES RIGHT TO LEFT

THE CHANGE OF PLACES LEFT TO RIGHT

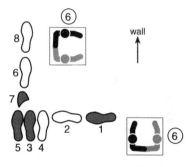

STEPS	**THE WALKS IN PROMENADE**	BEATS

Start position (feet not illustrated). Normal hold. Weight on RF.
(Facing wall.)

Four

1	Turn left side away from partner. LF back in fallaway position	*One
2	Replace weight onto RF, in PP. Start turning right	Two
3	LF diagonally forward along LOD, turning partner towards you	Three
4	Close RF part way to LF	a
5	LF diagonally forward along LOD	Four
6	RF forward and across, along LOD, partner turning into PP	*One
7	Close LF, on ball, part way to RF	a
8	RF forward and across, still in PP	Two

Either repeat steps 3–8 (6 steps = 2 chassés) *or* repeat step 3 followed by step 6 *twice* (4 steps). Follow with the Fallaway Throwaway or with the Change of Places Right to Left, both figures starting with step 3.

Three

Four

*One

Two

THE AMERICAN SPIN

Three

Precede with the Change of Places Right to Left or with the Change of Places Left to Right having switched to a handshake hold on the last step.

Four

Start position (feet not illustrated) facing partner. RF forward. Weight on RF. (Facing LOD.)

1	LF back	*One
2	Replace weight onto RF	Two
3	LF a very small step to the side, gently leading partner towards you	Three
4	RF a step in place, still leading partner towards you	a
5	LF a step in place. Brace your right arm	Four
	(Partner spins to her right as you release RH)	
6	RF a very small step to the side. Partner still turning	*One
7	LF a step in place. Partner still turning	a
8	RF a step in place. With RH catch your partner's RH	Two
	(to finish in handshake hold)	

Repeat steps 1–8 (as many times as you wish). Alternatively, on step 8, catch your partner's RH in your LH (one-hand hold) and follow with the Link Rock, or the Change of Places Left to Right.

THE WALKS IN PROMENADE

8 6 7 5 3 4 2 1

(13)

← LOD

12 11 10 9 8   alternative single steps

THE AMERICAN SPIN

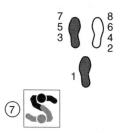

7
5
3

8
6
4
2

1

(7)

STEPS	**THE FALLAWAY ROCK**	BEATS

Start position (feet not illustrated). Normal hold. Weight on LF.
(Facing centre.)   Four

1	Turn right side away from partner. RF back in fallaway position. (Facing LOD)	*One
2	Replace weight onto LF, in PP. Start turning left	Two

3	RF a small step to the side, while turning left to face partner	Three
4	Close LF halfway to RF	a
5	RF a small step to the side	Four

6	LF a small step to the side	*One
7	Close RF halfway to LF	a
8	LF a small step to the side	Two

Either repeat these steps *or* follow with the Fallaway Throwaway.

Three

	THE FALLAWAY THROWAWAY	

Start position (feet not illustrated). Normal hold. Weight on LF.   Four
(Facing centre.)

1	Turn right side away from partner. RF back in fallaway position. (Facing LOD)	*One
2	Replace weight onto LF, in PP. Start turning left towards partner	Two

3	RF diagonally forward, still turning left, towards partner's left side	Three
4	Close LF a short way to RF, while turning left to face against LOD	a
5	RF a very small step to the side while swaying to right. (Lower RH slightly)	Four
6	LF a small step back on ball while recovering sway. Release RH	*One
7	Draw RF back halfway to LF	a
8	LF a small step back while extending right arm. (Now in open facing position)	Two

Dance a backward chassé, facing your partner on steps 6, 7 and 8.
Follow with the Link Rock.

THE FALLAWAY ROCK

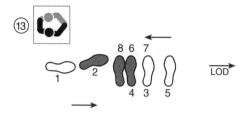

THE FALLAWAY THROWAWAY

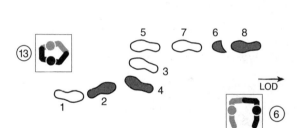

STEPS	**THE LINK ROCK**	BEATS

Start in open facing position (feet not illustrated). LF back. Weight on LF.
(Facing against LOD.)

Four

1	RF back	*One

2	Replace weight onto LF	Two

3	RF a small step forward. Moving towards partner	Three
4	Close LF, on ball, halfway to RF	a
5	RF a small step forward. Resume normal hold	Four

6	LF a small step to the side	*One
7	Close RF halfway to LF	a
8	LF a small step to the side	Two

Follow with the Fallaway Rock, the Fallaway Throwaway, the
Change of Places Right to Left or the Walks in Promenade.

Three

THE CHANGE OF HANDS BEHIND BACK

Start in open facing position (feet not illustrated). LF back. Weight on LF.
(Facing centre.)

Four

1	RF back	*One

2	Replace weight onto LF	Two

3	RF forward as partner leads you towards his right side	Three
4	Close LF, on ball, halfway to RF	a
5	RF forward, on partner's right, as he takes your RH in his RH	Four
	(As you pass behind your partner, he changes his hands behind his back)	
6	On RF swivel right to face partner. LF back (on ball). (Facing wall)	*One
7	Draw RF back halfway to LF	a
8	LF back. Extend RH as you move away into open facing position	Two

Either repeat these eight steps *or* dance the Link Rock or the Change of Places
Left to Right.

Three

Four

*One

Two

THE KICK BALL CHANGE

This 'figure', which can be danced in open facing or promenade position, is
an alternative way of dancing the first *two beats* of some figures by squeezing in
three steps instead of two. The rhythm is the same as in the chassés but the steps
and action are quite different.

Three

Four

1	Flick RF forward, from the knee, just clear of the floor	*One
2	RF, on ball, a small step back just behind LF	a
3	Replace weight onto LF	Two

THE LINK ROCK

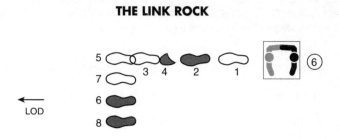

THE CHANGE OF HANDS BEHIND BACK

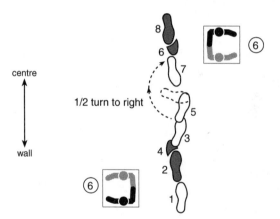

centre

wall

1/2 turn to right

THE KICK BALL CHANGE

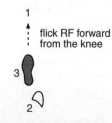

flick RF forward
from the knee

STEPS	**THE CHANGE OF PLACES RIGHT TO LEFT**	BEATS
	Start position (feet not illustrated). Normal hold. Weight on LF. (Facing centre.)	Four
1	Turn right side away from partner. RF back in fallaway position. (Facing LOD)	*One
2	Replace weight onto LF, in PP, start to turn left	Two
3	RF a small step to the side, while turning left to face partner	Three
4	Close LF halfway to RF	a
5	RF a small step to the side. Start turning right under raised RH	Four
6	Release LH. On RF swivel to right to face partner. LF back (on ball)	*One
7	Draw RF back halfway to LF. Lower RH. (Facing against LOD)	a
8	LF back. Extend RH as you move away into open facing position	Two

Follow with the Link Rock, the Change of Places Left to Right, the Change of Hands Behind Back or the American Spin.

THE CHANGE OF PLACES LEFT TO RIGHT

Start in open facing position (feet not illustrated). LF back. Weight on LF. (Facing against LOD.)

1	RF back	*One
2	Replace weight onto LF	Two
3	RF forward. Start to turn left. RH will be raised	Three
4	Close LF part way to RF, still turning under raised arm	a
5	RF a small step to side with your back towards your partner. (Facing DW)	Four
6	On RF swivel left to face partner. LF back (on ball). (Facing centre)	*One
7	Draw RF back halfway to LF. RH is lowered	a
8	LF back. Extend RH as you move into open facing position	Two

Follow with the Link Rock, the Change of Hands Behind Back or the American Spin.

THE CHANGE OF PLACES RIGHT TO LEFT

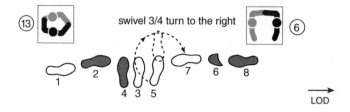

swivel 3/4 turn to the right

LOD

THE CHANGE OF PLACES LEFT TO RIGHT

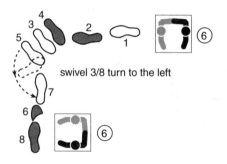

swivel 3/8 turn to the left

LOD

STEPS   **THE WALKS IN PROMENADE**   BEATS

Start position (feet not illustrated). Normal hold. Weight on LF.
(Facing centre.)   Four

1	Turn right side away from partner. RF back in fallaway position	*One
2	Replace weight onto LF, in PP. Start to turn left	Two
3	RF a small step to the side, turning left to face partner	Three
4	Close LF halfway to RF	a
5	RF a small step to the side. Start to turn right	Four
6	Turn right to face LOD. LF a small step forward in PP	*One
7	Close RF, on ball, halfway to LF	a
8	LF a small step forward, still in PP, start turning left	Two

Either repeat steps 3–8 (6 steps = 2 chassés) *or* repeat step 3 followed by
step 6 *twice* (4 steps). Follow with the Fallaway Throwaway or with the   Three
Change of Places Right to Left, both figures starting with step 3.

                                                                      Four

                                                                      *One

                                                                      Two

THE AMERICAN SPIN   Three

Precede with the Change of Places Right to Left or with the Change of Places
Left to Right having switched to a handshake hold on the last step.   Four
Start position (feet not illustrated) facing partner. LF back. Weight on LF.
(Facing against LOD.)

1	RF back	*One
2	Replace weight onto LF	Two
3	RF a small step forward towards partner	Three
4	Close LF, on ball, halfway to RF	a
5	RF a small step forward. Lean towards partner and brace arm	Four
	(When hold is released, spin on RF a half turn to right)	
6	Still turning right, LF a small step close to RF	*One
7	Still turning, replace weight onto RF	a
8	Now facing partner. Replace weight onto LF. Resume handshake hold	Two

Repeat steps 1–8 as many times as you wish. Alternatively, on step 8, your
partner catches your RH in his LH (one-hand hold) before following with the
Link Rock, or the Change of Places Left to Right.

THE WALKS IN PROMENADE

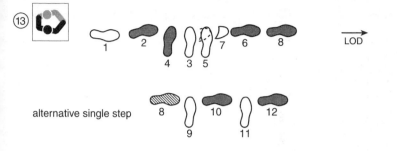

LOD

alternative single step

THE AMERICAN SPIN

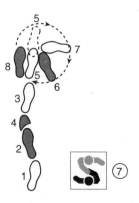

Perfecting your Jive technique

Starting

Having counted a bar or two, you may find it easier to dance the two chassés before moving back on step 1.

Footwork and Jive action

Except where instructed otherwise – and unless the tempo is quick – each step is taken ball flat, with the rhythm being felt mainly in the knees which, during the chassés, should be slightly flexed while you dance the first two steps and straightened during the third step as your hips swing over your supporting foot. During steps 1 and 2 of each figure, the foot, ankle, leg and knee action is the same as in the Cha-cha-cha. This action induces a natural hip-swing on these two steps and also on the last step of each chassé.

Unless the music's tempo is quick, the three steps of chassés which travel forward are danced ball flat, ball only, ball flat; but the steps of chassés which travel backwards are danced ball only, ball flat, ball flat. When the tempo is quick, *all* chassé steps are danced ball only, ball only, ball flat to enable you to dance in time with the music while retaining light, springy knees.

Arms

Free arms swing with the body in a natural, carefree manner but, when hands are joined, both partners' arms must be slightly braced so as to give – and respond to – leads. Hands should not be held tightly and wrists should not be tensed.

Partners' roles

The woman must follow her partner's leads and avoid anticipating his choreography. The Jive induces in a man the feeling of being on a vertical axis about which he leads and counterbalances his partner while tapping out the rhythm with small quick steps. To maintain his partner's balance, he must keep his raised hand above her head while she dances underarm turns.

Alternative choreographies

For the sake of clarity all figures in this chapter have been shown with their first steps being danced on beat one of a bar. In practice, because each figure requires 1½ bars of music, a *following* figure's first step must be danced on beat three. Consider, as an example, a routine comprising this chapter's first three figures: if the first step of the Fallaway Rock is danced on beat one, then the first step of the Fallaway Throwaway will be danced on beat three and the first step of the Link Rock will be danced on beat one.

a Jive Chassé to Left then Right (woman right then left).
Fallaway Throwaway.
Change of Hands Behind Back (twice).
Link Rock.

b Fallaway Rock.
Change of Places Right to Left.
Change of Places Left to Right.
Change of Hands Behind Back (twice).
Link Rock.

c Jive Chassé to Left and Right.
Fallaway Throwaway.
Change of Hands Behind Back. ⎫
Change of Places Left to Right. ⎬ repeat
                                          ⎭
American Spin.
Link Rock.

d Link Rock.
Walks in Promenade.
Kick Ball Change (twice).
Fallaway Throwaway steps 3–8.
Change of Hands Behind Back.
Change of Places Left to Right.
Link Rock.

e Walks in Promenade steps 1–8, then repeat steps 3 and 6 twice.
Change of Places Right to Left steps 3–8.
American Spin (twice).
Change of Places Left to Right.
Link Rock with the Kick Ball Change in place of steps 1 and 2.

10 | ROCK 'N' ROLL

Because the Rock 'n' Roll is a variant of the Jive it shares the Jive's early history and people still frequently claim to be dancing one when, in fact, they are dancing the other. It is a non-progressive dance and alignments on the following pages are only suggestions.

Harlem in the 1950s, the nursery of the Rock 'n' Roll, is evoked by *Blue Suede Shoes*, *Great Balls of Fire* and *Rock Around the Clock*; but travel changes dances even more than it changes people and the laid back Rock 'n' Roll, with its huge tempo range of 36 to 60 bars per minute, is extremely adaptable. It is a wonder then, that a true blue Harlem man, on holiday in Hong Kong, can recognize its carefree rhythm instantly – in spite of an unfamiliar melodic wrapping – and can feel at home beating it out with his feet while his partner spins, turns, jumps and passes behind his back.

Rock 'n' Roll music is in 4/4 time (four beats to each bar). The four-step pattern is danced to a *quick-quick-slow-slow* rhythm over six beats (1½ bars) of music. Read down the beat margin of the Rock Basic and you will see *one-two-three-four-one-two*. But, if you read further down, you will see two unused beats (*three-four*) with no steps because other items are in the way. When you are dancing, the music goes on and so do you, taking the first step of the next figure on beat *three* of the same bar. Each of the *slow* steps, marked **S** in the step-side margins of the following pages, is spread over two beats. Because its steps are relatively simple, beginners are often taught Rock 'n' Roll figures to introduce them, in an easy way, to the Jive. But the Rock 'n' Roll also adapts to the demands of competitors and medallists and is especially suitable for parties and social dancing because it can be danced in a very small space. It is an adaptable dance but emphatically not just 'a lazy man's Jive'. Many figures have versions for each dance and experienced dancers often flit from Jive to Rock 'n' Roll and back to Jive in the course of one sequence.

Practise the Rock Basic – keeping the steps small and the knees relaxed – until you can dance it accurately just by listening to the rhythm. Next dance a Rock Basic followed by a Throwaway and then another Rock Basic which is started in open facing position and finished in normal hold. Both partners should keep their arms relaxed while dancing these figures, except when it is time to give or receive a lead, when they must be braced. Master this short sequence before adding further figures.

Holds

The loose normal hold is the same as in the Jive. The Jive's one-hand hold (man's left, woman's right), handshake hold (man's right, woman's right) and double hold positions are also used frequently. Most figures on the following pages may be started and finished in double hold or one-hand hold instead of in normal hold.

Footwork

Footwork to be ball flat unless instructed otherwise.

Figure 10.1   Normal hold position

STEPS	**THE ROCK BASIC**	BEATS

Start position (feet not illustrated). Normal hold. Feet apart. Weight on RF.
(Facing wall.) — **Four**

1 Q Turn left side away from partner. LF back in fallaway position — ***One**

2 Q Replace weight onto RF, in PP. Start turning right — **Two**

3 S LF a small step to the side, while — **Three**

3 turning right to face partner — **Four**

4 S Transfer weight — ***One**

4 sideways onto RF — **Two**

Repeat these steps as many times as you wish. You may rotate the figure to the
right or to the left. If danced facing partner in one-hand hold or in double hold,
step 1 becomes – *LF back leading partner to step back* – (not in fallaway) thus
eliminating the turn into and out of PP. — **Three**

Four

*One

Two

Three

THE THROWAWAY — **Four**

Start position (including alternative holds) is the same as for the Rock Basic.

1 Q Turn left side away from partner. LF back in fallaway position — ***One**

2 Q Replace weight onto RF, in PP. Start turning left — **Two**

3 S LF a small step diagonally forward. Lower LH slightly while — **Three**

3 swaying to left and starting to turn left. Partner still facing you — **Four**

4 S RF a small side step while recovering sway to complete turn to — ***One**

4 face LOD. Lead partner to step back into open facing position — **Two**
(Release RH.)

You may dance this figure without turning left, but your partner *will* turn and
end the figure on your left side at a right angle to you. Follow with the Rock
Basic (to resume normal hold), the Woman's Underarm Turn to the Left, the
Change of Hands Behind Back or the Push Spin.

THE ROCK BASIC

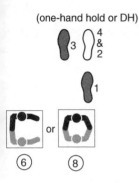

(one-hand hold or DH)

3 4 & 2

1

6 or 8

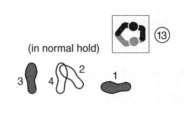

(in normal hold)

3 4 2 1

⑬

THE THROWAWAY

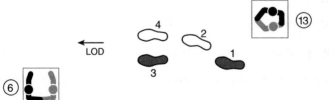

⑬

4 2 1

← LOD

3

⑥

STEPS **THE WOMAN'S UNDERARM TURN TO THE RIGHT** BEATS

Start position (feet not illustrated). Normal hold. Feet apart. Weight on RF.
(Facing wall.)

Four

| 1 | Q | Turn left side away from partner. LF back in fallaway position | *One |

| 2 | Q | Replace weight onto RF in PP | Two |

| 3 | | LF diagonally forward, starting to turn left | Three |
| 3 | S | Raise LH and lead partner to turn right, then release RH | Four |

| 4 | | Having completed turn, to face LOD, RF a very small step forward | *One |
| 4 | S | Lower LH as partner completes her turn into open facing position | Two |

You may dance this figure without turning left, but your partner *will* turn and
end the figure on your left side at a right angle to you. Follow with the Woman's
Underarm Turn to the Left.

Three

Four

*One

Two

Three

THE WOMAN'S UNDERARM TURN TO THE LEFT

Start in open facing position (feet not illustrated), RF forward. Weight on RF.
(Facing LOD.)

Four

| 1 | Q | LF a small step back. Lead partner to step back | *One |

| 2 | Q | Replace weight forward onto RF | Two |

| 3 | | While starting to turn right, close LF almost to RF and | Three |
| 3 | S | raise LH to lead partner across you to begin turning to her left | Four |

| 4 | | Complete turn to face wall. RF a small step to the side, then | *One |
| 4 | S | lower LH as partner completes her turn into open facing position | Two |

If you start with your partner at a right angle to you, dance the Rock Basic
without turning. Follow with the Rock Basic (to resume normal hold), the
Change of Hands Behind Back, the Windmill, or the Push Spin.

THE WOMAN'S UNDERARM TURN TO THE RIGHT

LOD

THE WOMAN'S UNDERARM TURN TO THE LEFT

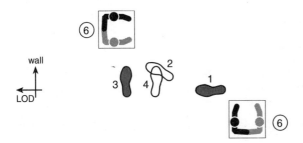

wall

LOD

STEPS   **THE CHANGE OF HANDS BEHIND BACK**   BEAT

Start in open facing position (feet not illustrated). RF forward. Weight on RF.
(Facing wall.)

1	Q LF a small step back. Lead partner to step back	*On
2	Q Replace weight onto RF	Tw
3	LF forward. Start to turn left while leading partner	Three
3 S	to pass on your right side. Place RH over her RH	Fou
4	Change hands behind your back while completing a half turn	*On
4 S	to the left to face centre. RF back into open facing position	Tw

Either repeat this figure *or* follow with the Woman's Underarm Turn to the Left.

Three

THE PUSH SPIN

Start in open facing position (feet not illustrated), in handshake hold. Feet apart.   Fou
Weight on RF.

1	Q LF a small step back, leading partner to step back	*On
2	Q Replace weight onto RF	Tw
3 S	LF a small step to the side, leading partner towards you. Brace	Three
3 S	right arm and with RH, spin partner to her right then release	Fou
4 S	Replace weight onto RF. With RH catch your partner's RH	*On
4 S	(handshake hold) as she completes her turn	Tw

Either repeat this figure in handshake hold, *or* in one-hand hold *or* follow with
the Woman's Underarm Turn to the Left (having changed to one-hand hold).
As a surprise, your partner may lead you to spin a full left turn on step 3 while
she dances the Rock Basic.

THE CHANGE OF HANDS BEHIND BACK

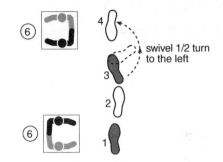

centre

wall

swivel 1/2 turn
to the left

THE PUSH SPIN

STEPS	**THE WINDMILL**	BEATS
Start facing partner (feet not illustrated). Feet apart. Weight on RF. Double hold (maintained throughout the figure).		Four

1 Q LF a small step back, leading partner to step back   *One

2 Q Replace weight onto RF   Two

3 S Start turning left. LF a small step forward while swaying left   Three

3 Open lower arms to lead partner towards your left side   Four

4 S Swivel up to a half turn. RF a small step to the side.   *One

4 Recover sway while closing arms to lead partner to step back   Two

Repeat as you wish or, while stepping forward with your LF, sway and turn to your *right* while leading partner towards your right side. Follow with the   Three

Throwaway, or the Woman's Underarm Turn to the Right – but, if *you* turn right,   Four

follow with the Woman's Underarm Turn to the Left.   *One

    Two

    Three

AN ALTERNATE STYLE – THE TAP BASIC   Four

Start positions are the same as in the Rock Basic.

1 Q Turn left side away from partner. LF back in fallaway position   *One

2 Q Replace weight onto RF, in PP. Start turning right   Two

3 Q Tap LF (on ball) to the side turning right to face partner   Three

4 Q LF a small step to the side with full weight   Four

5 Q Tap RF (on ball) to the side   *One

6 Q RF a small step to the side with full weight   Two

The Tap Basic is really an alternative way to dance the Rock Basic and the Rock Basic's footnote applies to it. Equivalent tap steps may be danced on all slow counts in the figures in this chapter.

THE WINDMILL

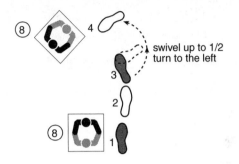

AN ALTERNATE STYLE – THE TAP BASIC

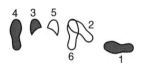

STEPS   **THE ROCK BASIC**   BEAT

Start position (feet not illustrated). Normal hold. Feet apart. Weight on LF.
(Facing centre.)   Fou

1 Q Turn right side away from partner. RF back in fallaway position   *One

2 Q Replace weight onto LF, in PP. Start turning left   Tw

3 S RF a small step to the side, while   Three

3 S turning left to face partner   Fou

4 S Transfer weight   *One

4 S sideways onto LF   Two

Repeat these steps as many times as you wish. You may rotate the figure to the
right or to the left. If danced facing partner in one-hand hold or in double hold, Three
step 1 becomes – *RF back still facing partner* – (not in fallaway) thus eliminating
the turn into and out of PP.   Fou

                                          *One

                                        Two

                                        Three

         THE THROWAWAY   Four

Start position (including alternative holds) is the same as for the Rock Basic.

1 Q Turn right side away from partner. RF back in fallaway position   *One

2 Q Replace weight onto LF, in PP. Start turning left   Two

3 S Your partner will lead you to turn left and step RF   Three

3 S sideways around him towards his left side, while swaying right Four

4 S Complete turn while recovering sway, to face against LOD. Release *One

4 S LH. Right arm extends as you step LF back into open facing position Two

Your steps do not change if your partner dances without turning, *but* you will
finish at a right angle to his left side. Follow with the Rock Basic (to resume
normal hold), the Woman's Underarm Turn to the Left, the Change of Hands
Behind Back or the Push Spin.

THE ROCK BASIC

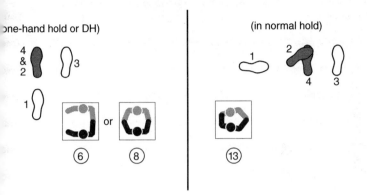

THE THROWAWAY

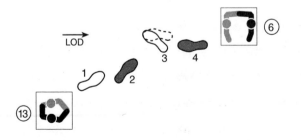

STEPS **THE WOMAN'S UNDERARM TURN TO THE RIGHT**   BEATS

Start position (feet not illustrated). Normal hold. Feet apart. Weight on LF.
(Facing centre.)   Four

1 Q Turn right side away from partner. RF back in fallaway position	***One**
2 Q Replace weight onto LF into PP	**Two**
3 RF to side, having turned left to face partner. Release LH as	**Three**
3 S you start turning right under your raised RH	**Four**
4 On RF swivel three-quarters of a turn to the right to face partner	***One**
4 S Your right arm is lowered. Step LF back into open facing position	**Two**

Your steps do not change if your partner dances without turning, *but* you will
finish at a right angle to his left side. Follow with the Woman's Underarm   **Three**
Turn to the Left.

Four

*One

Two

Three

THE WOMAN'S UNDERARM TURN TO THE LEFT

Start in open facing position (feet not illustrated), LF back. Weight on LF.   **Four**
(Facing against LOD.)

1 Q RF a small step back	***One**
2 Q Replace weight onto LF	**Two**
3 RF forward as your RH is raised, to lead you to turn left. Finish	**Three**
3 S with feet apart and your back towards partner. (Facing DW)	**Four**
4 On RF swivel left to face partner. (Facing centre)	***One**
4 S As right arm extends, step LF back into open facing position	**Two**

Your steps do not change if you start at a right angle to your partner. Follow
with the Rock Basic (to resume normal hold), the Change of Hands Behind
Back, the Windmill, or the Push Spin.

THE WOMAN'S UNDERARM TURN TO THE RIGHT

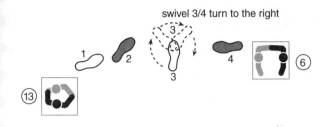

THE WOMAN'S UNDERARM TURN TO THE LEFT

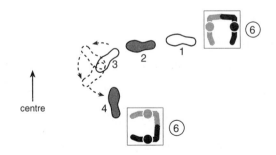

STEPS **THE CHANGE OF HANDS BEHIND THE BACK**

BEATS

Start in open facing position (feet not illustrated), LF back. Weight on LF.
(Facing centre.)

Four

1 Q RF a small step back

*One

2 Q Replace weight onto LF

Two

3 S RF forward towards partner's right side. Start to turn right

Three

3 S behind his back as he holds your RH in his RH

Four

4 S As you complete a half turn to the right, he will change hands

*One

4 S while you step LF back into open facing position

Two

Either repeat this figure *or* follow with the Woman's Underarm Turn to the Left.

Three

THE PUSH SPIN

Start in open facing position (feet not illustrated), in handshake hold.
Feet apart. Weight on LF.

Four

1 Q RF a small step back

*One

2 Q Replace weight onto LF

Two

3 S RF forward. With right arm braced, press RH against partner's RH

Three

3 S Release hold when he leads you to spin to your right

Four

4 S Having completed a full turn to face partner,

*One

4 S LF a small step back. Resume handshake hold

Two

Repeat as you wish or, if your partner changes hands, follow with the Woman's
Underarm Turn to the Left unless he leads you, with his left hand, into another Push
Spin. For fun, dance the Rock Basic but, with your RH, spin your partner to his left
on step 3.

THE CHANGE OF HANDS BEHIND THE BACK

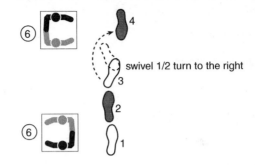

centre

wall

swivel 1/2 turn to the right

THE PUSH SPIN

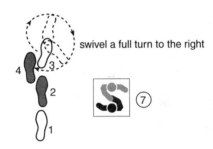

swivel a full turn to the right

STEPS	**THE WINDMILL**	BEATS

Start facing partner (feet not illustrated). Feet apart.
Weight on LF in double hold (maintained throughout figure). **Four**

1 Q RF a small step back ***One**

2 Q Replace weight onto LF **Two**

3 S Your arms will be extended to lead you to turn left and step RF **Three**

3 S sideways towards your partner's left side while also swaying right **Four**

4 S Swivel up to a half turn. Step LF back while recovering sway ***One**

4 S as your arms are returned to normal double hold position **Two**

Repeat, or alternatively, on step 3, step RF forward towards your partner's right
side, while turning to the right. Follow with the Throwaway, or the Woman's **Three**
Underarm Turn to the Right – but, if *you* turn right, follow with the Woman's
Underarm Turn to the Left. **Four**

*One

Two

Three

AN ALTERNATE STYLE – THE TAP BASIC **Four**

Start positions are the same as in the Rock Basic.

1 Q Turn right side away from partner. RF back in fallaway position ***One**

2 Q Replace weight onto LF, in PP. Start turning left **Two**

3 Q Tap RF (on ball) to the side turning left to face partner **Three**

4 Q RF a small step to the side with full weight **Four**

5 Q Tap LF (on ball) to the side ***One**

6 Q LF a small step to the side with full weight **Two**

The Tap Basic is really an alternative way to dance the Rock Basic and the
Rock Basic's footnote applies to it. Equivalent tap steps may be danced on all
slow counts in the figures in this chapter.

THE WINDMILL

Turn up to 1/2 turn to the left

AN ALTERNATE STYLE – THE TAP BASIC

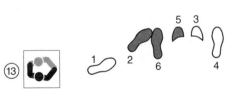

Perfecting your Rock 'n' Roll technique

Starting

The Rock 'n' Roll beat is usually emphatic, which makes starting easy but, if you start your first figure on beat one then you will begin your second figure (quite unconsciously) on beat three. Take the first three figures described in this chapter as an example: if you start the first Rock Basic on beat one, you will begin the Throwaway on beat three of the next bar and the second Rock Basic on beat one of the following bar.

Start by stepping off on beat one, *either* with a quick backwards step 1 (as shown) *or*, as some dancers prefer, with a **slow** sideways step 3 – whichever your teacher suggests – but count yourself in first, over a bar or two, and keep your partner in the picture.

Footwork

No matter what dance position you may be in, your first *quick* step in any figure is *always* back and your second *quick* step is *always* forward. When you are facing your partner with a hand hold, there is *always* a pulling-apart feeling on the first *quick* step.

Keep your steps small – tempos are often quick – and feel the rhythm in your flexed knees.

The Rock 'n' Roll is a *do-what-feels-comfortable* dance. Ball flat footwork is usual but the heel need not be lowered when you step back. You may step forward heel flat in some styles of the dance; and you may tap with the toe, the ball, or the heel, when you dance tap-step style – whichever comes most naturally.

Arms

Your free arm should swing in a natural, carefree manner. Joined hands should be held firmly with relaxed wrists and, when leads are to be given or taken, arms should be slightly braced.

Partner's roles

The man must lead and the woman must refrain from anticipating his choreography. When dancing underarm turns, the man must raise and lower his partner's hand at exactly the right times and, to maintain her balance, he must hold it directly above her head while she is turning.

Rock 'n' Roll styles

The simplest styles are the Rock Basic and the Tap Basic, described previously, which belong to the *Authentic* category of styles. The Tap Basic may be developed by dancing a heel-tap ball change in place of steps 1 and 2*, followed by a small sliding action before each of the other steps to produce a $1^1/2$ bar pattern of *one-a-two-a-three-a-four-a-one-a-two*. There are other styles in the (mainly European) *International* category which are used worldwide in medal tests and competitions. Because flicks, hops and jumps are added to the basic step patterns, couples dancing these styles adopt a more upright stance. At the competitive level they may be mistaken for acrobats.

Alternative choreographies

a Rock Basic.
Throwaway.
Change of Hands Behind
    Back.
Woman's Underarm Turn to
    Left.
Change of Hands Behind
    Back.
Woman's Underarm Turn to
    Left.
Rock Basic return to normal
    hold.

b Underarm Turn to Right.
Underarm Turn to Left.
Windmill to the left.
Windmill to the right.
Push Spin leading with LH.
Man's Push Spin to left.

c Underarm Turn to Right.
Push Spin.
Underarm Turn to Left.
Rock Basic return to normal
    hold.

d Push Spin, then regain
    handshake hold, and
    dance
Change of Hands Behind
    Back, turning $1/4$ to left
    (Woman to right)
    finishing with partner on
    Man's left side, both
    facing the same way.
    Hands still held behind
    the man's back.
Place LH on partner's
    shoulder and lead her
    into a Push Spin to right
    (Shoulder Spin.)
Finish facing each other.

*Similar to the Kick Ball Change in the Jive.

11 | ARGENTINE TANGO

Authorities responsible for the world's great ports have, in general, understood the importance of providing refreshment and relaxation for visiting seafarers and have encouraged the establishment of bars, brothels and cafés within easy walking distance of the quays.

> They towed her in to Liverpool, we made the hooker fast,
> And the copper-bound officials paid the crew,
> And Billy drew his money, but the money didn't last,
> For he painted the alongshore blue . . .
> It was rum for Poll, and rum for Nan, and gin for Jolly Jack.
> He shipped a week later in the clothes upon his back,
> He had to pinch a little straw, he had to beg a sack
> To sleep on, when his watch was through . . .
>
> *John Masefield*

Few authorities were more diligent in this respect than the city fathers of Buenos Aires. However, during the second half of the nineteenth century, their port and town were all but overwhelmed by a flood of immigrants. Young men, mainly from war-torn Italy and Spain, with a sprinkling of refugees from slave-dependent Caribbean countries, competed with visiting sailormen for the favours of the port's women and were united with the city's native poor in their kingdom of despair.

But Latins always dance, and there was no shortage of dances, or of music to dance to – from the old world and the new – played on guitars, violins and bandoneons (squeeze boxes with keyboards for each hand). Usually men danced in pairs or groups to attract one of the tiny minority of women but occasionally, if a man expressed his desire by dancing seductively enough – or if he had money – he might, with luck, dance *with* a woman.

By the end of the century, the original tango, the Argentine Tango, had developed from the lively Milonga – an Afro-Latin festival dance – to become the dance-language in which the poor people of Buenos Aires expressed themselves.

During most of the twentieth century the dance has been in purdah. Because of its eroticism, it was banned when it spread into middle-class Argentina. Europe and the US gentrified it, made it elegant, called it the Tango and promoted it as a ballroom dance. Now, a hundred years later, it is being revived on both sides of the Atlantic in its original form.

Argentine Tango music is in 4/4 time (four beats to each bar). Tempos vary, but a slow 27–30 bars per minute rate is appropriate if the dance's smooth, precise, cat-like character is to be expressed.

Comparisons with other Latin or ballroom dances are meaningless. The Argentine Tango is a one-off. It has no strict rhythm. It is always danced in normal hold by couples travelling slowly around the dance floor in an anti-clockwise direction; but their progress is interrupted frequently for turns, swivels, leg flicks and hooks and, because of these, the alignments indicated in this chapter are suggestions only.

The Reverse Basic, the first eight-step figure, is the framework into which the chapter's other figures can be fitted. Learn it thoroughly, at both suggested timings, before tackling the next figure, and try to keep your shoulders parallel to your partner's throughout the dance.

Normal hold

The hold is close because the man leads with body movements rather than with his arms. He stands upright with his weight forward over the balls of his feet. His partner tilts forward from her ankles, holding her straight body just apart from his while resting her left hand on his shoulder or draping it round his neck, as she pleases. She is supported by his right hand, well around her waist, and by their joined hands which are held at about his eye level. Arms are braced and elbows are held close. Partners make eye contact during swivels but at other times the woman's head is turned to the right and she looks downwards, over her shoulder.

Footwork

Forward steps are taken with a heel lead; all other steps are taken ball flat unless instructed otherwise.

Figure 11.1   Normal hold position

Figure 11.2   Outside partner position

Figure 11.3   Woman's flick in Forward Ocho

STEPS	**THE REVERSE BASIC (SALIDA)**	BEATS

Start position (feet illustrated). Feet together. Weight on LF.
Normal hold. (Facing LOD.) — **Four**

1 S	RF a short	*One
1	step back	Two
2 S	LF to the side *without turn*	Three
2	(further than your partner's step)	Four
3 S	With your left side leading, RF forward across LF (outside partner)	*One
3	(This is contrary body movement position – CBMP)	Two
4 S	Still with your left side leading,	Three
4	LF forward	Four
5 S	Close RF	*One
5	to LF	Two
6 S	LF	Three
6	forward	Four
7 S	RF	*One
7	to the side	Two
8 S	Close LF	Three
8	precisely to RF	Four

These eight steps may be repeated. Having practised dancing this figure with
eight *slow* steps over four bars of music, why not try dancing it over three bars
of music, by inserting four *quick* steps thus: *slow-slow-slow-quick-quick-
quick-quick-slow*? The Reverse Basic is the dance's travelling figure.
You may dance a quarter of a turn to the left during its last three steps (6, 7 and 8).
As you progress round the dance floor, you can fit each of the other figures
in this chapter into its eight steps. On a crowded floor you may delete step 1.
(The figure then becomes the Side Basic.)

THE REVERSE BASIC (SALIDA)

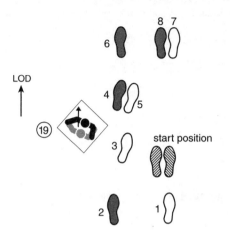

STEPS	**LA CUNITA (THE CRADLE)**	BEATS

Precede with steps 1–5 of the Reverse Basic.
Start position (feet not illustrated). Feet together. Weight on RF.

Four

Normal hold. (Facing LOD.)

1 Q LF forward while turning slightly left to be almost hip to hip   ***One**

2 Q Tap toe of RF across and behind LF   **Two**

3 Q RF back   **Three**

4 Q Tap toe LF across and in front of RF   **Four**

You will become conscious of a rocking motion if you repeat this figure.
You can sometimes manoeuvre into a space by rotating the figure gently   ***One**
anti-clockwise. Follow with steps 6–8 of the Reverse Basic.

Two

THE FORWARD OCHO (EIGHT)   **Three**

Precede with steps 1–5 of the Reverse Basic.
Start position (feet illustrated). Feet together. Weight on RF.   **Four**
Normal hold. (Facing LOD.)

1 S LF back, turning partner slightly to her left as she steps   ***One**

1 S outside your right side. Then turn her to her right into PP   **Two**

2 S Close RF to LF. Lead partner to step across   **Three**

2 S in front of you, turning her to her left to face you   **Four**

This figure may be repeated and, if you wish, rotated gently anti-clockwise.
Keep arms and shoulders braced to lead your partner in a figure of eight pattern
in front of you. Beginning the figure after step 3 or step 7 of the Reverse
Basic makes a change and is even easier.
Follow with steps 6–8 of the Reverse Basic.

LA CUNITA (THE CRADLE)

LOD

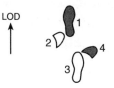

THE FORWARD OCHO (EIGHT)

start position after steps
4 & 5 of Reverse Basic

STEPS	**THE BACK OCHO**	BEATS

Precede with steps 1–3 of the Reverse Basic danced *slow-quick-quick* but, on step 3, close RF to LF and turn partner to her left so that her right side is towards you. Start position (feet illustrated). Feet together. Weight on RF. Normal hold in CPP. (Facing LOD.)

Three

Four

1 S	LF to the side leading partner to follow you by stepping back, then	*One
1	brush RF against LF and turn partner to her right	Two
	(Her left side is towards you)	
2 S	RF to the side leading partner to follow you by stepping back	Three
2	Brush LF against RF and turn partner to her left	Four
	(Her right side is towards you again)	

This figure may be repeated. Keep arms and shoulders braced to lead your partner in a figure of eight in front of you. To quit this figure, step LF forward then RF outside your partner, (slow, slow) quickly close LF to RF without weight and then dance steps 6–8 of the Reverse Basic.

*One

Two

STEPS	**THE SMALL RIGHT TURN (GIRO)**	**Three**

Precede with steps 1–5 of the Reverse Basic but cross RF on ball behind LF on step 5. Start position (feet illustrated). Feet crossed. Weight on LF. Normal hold. (Facing LOD.)

Four

1 S	Start turning slowly right on both feet, while leading partner	*One
1	to step forward on your right, to begin circling round you	Two
2 S	Continue turning right. Your feet begin to uncross as you	Three
2	lead your partner to zig-zag round you	Four
3 S	Continue turning right still leading your	*One
3	partner to zig-zag round you	Two
4 S	Finish with RF crossed in front. Weight on RF	Three
4	having completed a full turn	Four

You may turn a little less or a little more than a full turn.
Follow by stepping LF back into the Forward Ocho then dance steps 6–8 of the Reverse Basic.

THE BACK OCHO

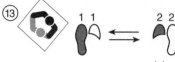

(also start position after
1 - 3 of Reverse Basic)

THE SMALL RIGHT TURN (GIRO)

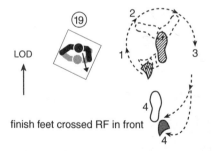

LOD

finish feet crossed RF in front

STEPS	**THE SMALL LEFT TURN (GIRO)**	BEATS

Precede with steps 1–3 of the Reverse Basic.
Start position (RF illustrated). RF outside partner. Weight on RF.
Normal hold. (Facing against LOD.)

1 S	Cross LF on ball behind RF. Lead partner to step towards your	*One
1	left side to begin circling round you	Two

2 S	Start turning left. Your feet begin to uncross as	Three
2	you lead your partner to zig-zag round you	Four

3 S	Complete your turn. Finish with weight on LF	*One
3	Partner still zig-zagging round you	Two

4 S	RF forward outside partner while	Three
4	leading her to step back. Now facing LOD	Four

The turn should be *approximately* one half turn.
Follow with steps 4–8 of the Reverse Basic or with La Cunita.   *One

EL GANCHO (THE HOOK)   Two

Precede with steps 1–3 of the Reverse Basic danced *slow-quick-quick*, but,
on step 3, close RF to LF and turn partner to her left so that her right   Three
side is towards you.
Start position (feet illustrated). Feet together. Weight on RF.   Four
Normal hold in CPP. (Facing LOD.)

1 S	LF diagonally forward, with knee bent, turning partner to her	*One
1	left. She then hooks her right leg round your left leg	Two

2 S	Transfer weight back onto RF before closing LF to RF with pressure	Three
2	while leading partner across to your right (into the Forward Ocho)	Four

3 S	Stand still with feet together. Lead partner to	*One
3	turn to her left (to complete her Forward Ocho)	Two

Follow with another Forward Ocho or steps 6–8 of the Reverse Basic.
Note: on step 1 your partner may choose to cross her RF in front of her left
leg instead of hooking her right leg round your left leg.

THE SMALL LEFT TURN (GIRO)

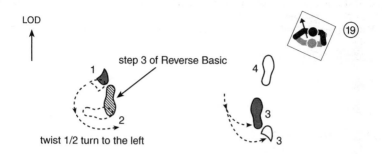

LOD

step 3 of Reverse Basic

twist 1/2 turn to the left

EL GANCHO (THE HOOK)

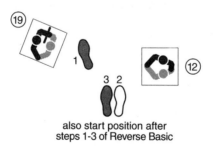

also start position after
steps 1-3 of Reverse Basic

STEPS	**THE TURNING REVERSE BASIC**	BEATS

Dance this version of the Reverse Basic when you are **not** facing the LOD.

Start position (feet not illustrated). Weight on LF.

Normal hold. (Facing against LOD.)

1 **S**	RF back down LOD	*One
1	start turning left	Two
2 **S**	Having turned a quarter left (to face wall)	Three
2	LF to the side	Four
3 **S**	Having turned left a further quarter (to face LOD) with	*One
3	your left side leading, RF forward outside partner in CBMP	Two
4 Q	LF forward (still facing LOD)	Three
5 Q	Close RF to LF	Four
6 Q	LF forward, start turning left	*One
7 Q	Having turned a quarter left (to face centre), RF to the side	Two
8 **S**	Having turned left a further quarter (to face against LOD), with	Three
8	your right side leading, LF back – partner now outside in CBMP	Four

Follow with another Turning Reverse Basic or with the Forward Ocho.

Note: You may dance steps 1–5 of the Turning Reverse Basic followed by steps 6–8 of the Reverse Basic to finish facing LOD. Remember there is no set rhythm, so that all the steps may be danced as slow counts.

THE TURNING REVERSE BASIC

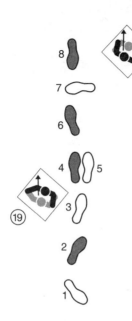

LOD

wall

STEPS	**THE REVERSE BASIC (SALIDA)**	BEATS

Start position (feet illustrated). Feet together. Weight on RF.
Normal hold. (Facing against LOD.)   **Four**

1	LF a short	*One
1	step forward	Two
2	RF to the side	Three
2	(shorter than your partner's step)	Four
3	With your shoulders parallel to your partner's,	*One
3	LF back (with your partner outside you on your right)	Two
4	Still with your shoulders parallel,	Three
4	RF back (on ball)	Four
5	Cross LF loosely, with weight,	*One
5	in front of RF	Two
6	RF	Three
6	back	Four
7	LF	*One
7	to the side	Two
8	Close RF	Three
8	precisely to LF	Four

These eight steps may be repeated. Having practised dancing this figure with
eight *slow* steps over four bars of music, why not try dancing it over three
bars of music, by inserting four *quick* steps thus: *slow-slow-slow-quick-quick-
quick-quick-slow*? The Reverse Basic is the dance's travelling figure.
You may dance a quarter of a turn to the left during its last three steps (6, 7 and 8).
As you progress round the dance floor, you can fit each of the other figures in
this chapter into its eight steps. On a crowded floor you may delete step 1.
(The figure then becomes the Side Basic.)

THE REVERSE BASIC (SALIDA)

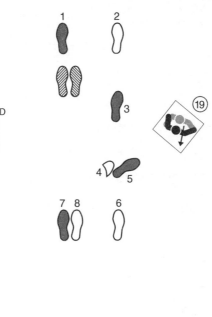

LOD

STEPS	**LA CUNITA (THE CRADLE)**	BEATS

Precede with steps 1–5 of the Reverse Basic.

Start position (feet not illustrated). Feet crossed. Weight on LF. **Four**

Normal hold. (Facing against LOD.)

1	Q RF back, partner on right almost hip to hip	*One

2	Q Tap toe of LF across and in front of RF	Two

3	Q LF forward	Three

4	Q Tap toe of RF across and behind LF	Four

You will become conscious of a rocking motion if you repeat this figure.

You can sometimes manoeuvre into a space by rotating the figure gently ***One**
anti-clockwise. Follow with steps 6–8 of the Reverse Basic.

Two

THE FORWARD OCHO (EIGHT)   Three

Precede with steps 1–5 of the Reverse Basic. Start position (feet illustrated).

Feet crossed. Weight on LF. Normal hold. (Facing against LOD.) **Four**

Before taking step 1, flick RF back and up while swivelling left.

1 S	RF forward outside partner, keeping your shoulders parallel to	*One

1	his, and flick LF back and up while swivelling right into PP	Two

2 S	LF forward (in PP) in front of partner, and swivel left	Three

2	to finish facing him while closing RF, without weight, to LF	Four

Note: while swivelling, you may close your free foot neatly instead of flicking it.
This figure may be repeated and rotated gently anti-clockwise as you swivel in
a figure of eight in front of your partner. If you begin this figure after step
3 or step 7 of the Reverse Basic, omit the flick and swivel which precede
step 1. Follow with steps 6–8 of the Reverse Basic.

PP = In FROSS
of no
partner

LA CUNITA (THE CRADLE)

THE FORWARD OCHO (EIGHT)

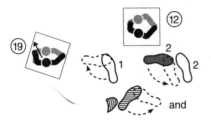

LOD

Right Foot Forward

From

STEPS **THE BACK OCHO** BEAT

Precede with steps 1–3 of the Reverse Basic danced *slow-quick-quick* but,
on step 3, close LF to RF without weight while turning left so that your right **Three**
side is towards your partner. Start position (feet illustrated).

Feet together. Weight on RF. Normal hold in CPP. (Facing wall.) **Four**

1 S LF back then swivel on it for up to a half turn to the right,	*One
1 while drawing RF to it without weight	Two
2 S RF back then swivel on it for a quarter turn to the left to	Three
2 face partner, while drawing LF to it without weight	Four

If this figure is repeated, increase your swivel on step 2 to a half turn. While
you dance the figure of eight in front of your partner, keep your shoulders *One
as parallel as possible to his. Follow with steps 3 to 8 of the Reverse Basic.

Two

THE SMALL RIGHT TURN (GIRO)

Precede with steps 1–5 of the Reverse Basic. Three

Start position (feet not illustrated). Feet crossed. Weight on LF.

Normal hold. (Facing against LOD.) Four

Before taking step 1, flick RF back and up while swivelling left.

1 S RF forward outside partner	*One
1 starting to turn right	Two
2 S Turn right for a half turn and	Three
2 step to the side with LF	Four
3 S Continue turning for just under a half turn and	*One
3 step back with RF	Two
4 S LF to the side	Three
4 as turn is completed	Four

You dance a zig-zag or *grapevine* round your partner. Take long, slow steps
while keeping your shoulders parallel to his. You may turn a little less
or a little more than a full turn. Follow with the Forward Ocho then
dance steps 6–8 of the Reverse Basic.

THE BACK OCHO

swivel to the left   swivel to the right

LOD

THE SMALL RIGHT TURN (GIRO)

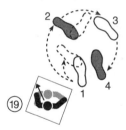

STEPS	**THE SMALL LEFT TURN (GIRO)**	BEATS

Precede with steps 1–3 of the Reverse Basic.

Start position (LF illustrated). LF back (partner outside). Weight on LF. **Four**
Normal hold. (Facing LOD.)

1 S	RF	*One
1	to the side	Two

2 S	LF forward, outside partner's left side	Three
2	while starting to turn left	Four

3 S	Having turned left about a quarter turn,	*One
3	step to the side with RF	Two

4 S	Turn left another quarter turn – to face against LOD –	Three
4	then step back with LF. (Partner outside)	Four

You dance a zig-zag or *grapevine* round your partner. Take long, slow steps
while keeping your shoulders parallel to his. The turn should be *approximately* ***One**
one half turn. Follow with steps 4–8 of the Reverse Basic or with La Cunita.

EL GANCHO (THE HOOK)   **Two**

Precede with steps 1–3 of the Reverse Basic danced *slow-quick-quick*, but,
on step 3, close LF to RF without weight while turning left so that your right **Three**
side is towards your partner.

Start position (feet illustrated). Feet together. Weight on RF. **Four**
Normal hold in CPP. (Facing wall.)

1 S	Turn slightly left. Step back with LF and flex knee	*One
1	Flick RF up and back (hook) between partner's legs	Two

2 S	RF forward outside partner, keeping your shoulders parallel to his	Three
2	and flick LF back and up while swivelling right into PP	Four

3 S	LF forward (in PP) in front of partner and swivel left to	*One
3	finish facing partner while closing RF without weight to LF	Two

(Steps 2 and 3 are the same as the two steps of the Forward Ocho.)
To give your partner time to position himself, your hooking flick must be
danced at the *end* of beat 2. You may, as an alternative, cross your
RF just above the knee of your left leg. Follow with the Forward Ocho or
with steps 6–8 of the Reverse Basic. Keep your knees together while you
flick/hook your right leg.

THE SMALL LEFT TURN (GIRO)

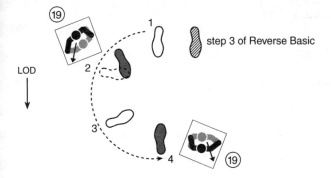

step 3 of Reverse Basic

LOD

EL GANCHO (THE HOOK)

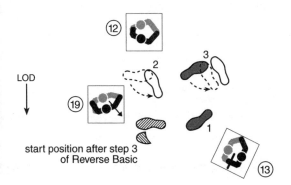

start position after step 3
of Reverse Basic

LOD

STEPS	**THE TURNING REVERSE BASIC**	BEAT!

Dance this version of the Reverse Basic when the previous figure has turned you to face LOD. Start position (feet not illustrated). Weight on RF. Normal hold. (Facing LOD.) | | **Four**

1 S	LF forward down LOD,	*One
1	start turning left	Two
2 S	Having turned a quarter left (to face centre)	Three
2	RF to the side	Four
3 S	Having turned left a further quarter (to face against LOD) with	*One
3	your right side slightly back, LF back. Partner now outside in CBMP	Two
4	Q RF back on ball, with right side still back	Three
5	Q Cross LF loosely with weight in front of RF	Four
6	Q RF back, start turning left	*One
7	Q Having turned a quarter left (to face wall), LF to the side	Two
8 S	Having turned a further quarter (to face LOD), with left side leading,	Three
8	RF forward across LF (outside partner)	Four

(This is contrary body movement position – CBMP)

Follow with another Turning Reverse Basic or with the Forward Ocho.

Note: You may dance steps 1–5 of the Turning Reverse Basic followed by steps 6–8 of the Reverse Basic to finish facing against LOD. Remember there is no set rhythm, so that all the steps may be danced as slow counts.

THE TURNING REVERSE BASIC

LOD

start facing LOD

1

2

3

4 5

6

7

8

(19)

(19)

centre

Perfecting your Argentine Tango techniqu

Starting

Although not as dominant as the ballroom Tangos, the beat of th
Argentine Tango is still emphatic and its bar-related music
phrasing makes it easy to identify the first beat. Count yourself i
over a bar or two, then step off on beat one – or, if the floor
crowded, start with a sidestep on beat two. Be careful when buyin
recordings. Some are hopeless for dancing because they hav
varying tempos.

Footwork and style

Take each step by positioning your foot deliberately befor
transferring weight onto it. On a slow count you will appear to b
feeling your way gingerly before committing yourself. Forwar
steps are taken with a heel lead but, on side and closing steps, th
ball of your foot must skim the floor, as it moves into position
before your heel is lowered. Your moving foot must brush you
supporting foot when you take a forward or backward step. Whe
the step begins with the feet apart, the foot's path is L-shaped;
closes, brushes the supporting foot, then moves forwards o
backwards. When the step will end with the feet apart, the foot
path is still L-shaped; it moves forwards or backwards, brushing th
supporting foot, then moves to the side. When you step outside you
partner, with one side of your body leading, the foot you are movin
forwards or backwards is placed on the line of the supporting foot
As you transfer weight to it, you will be aware that your uppe
thighs are crossed. This is called *contrary body movement positio*
(CBMP).

Couples have a dream-like appearance as they move slowly along
the line of dance. Their upper bodies are still. Their deliberate step
just skim the floor. The man holds his partner with brace
motionless arms and leads her with gentle turning movements of hi
body. Then comes an explosion. The woman turns, flicks or hook
her leg.

The Argentine Tango is woven around the woman's brief
spectacular displays. She is the queen of the dance.

lternative choreographies

1–5 Reverse Basic.
La Cunita.
6–8 Reverse Basic.

1–3 Reverse Basic (SQQ).
Back Ocho.
El Gancho (Hook).
Forward Ocho (twice).
6–8 Reverse Basic.

c 1–5 Reverse Basic.
Small Right Turn (Giro).
Forward Ocho.
Steps 6 and 7 Reverse
    Basic.
Forward Ocho.
6–8 Reverse Basic.

d 1–3 Reverse Basic.
Small Left Turn (Giro).
La Cunita (twice).
The man quickly swings LF
    round RF to step back
    while swivelling his
    partner to her left into
    the Forward Ocho
    (twice).
6–8 Reverse Basic.

ORGANIZATIONS WORLDWIDE

Wherever you travel, there is likely to be a national danc
organization which can tell you about dancing schools in your are
The list which follows covers 48 countries.

Australia   Australian Dancing Board, Mr Derek Gatley,
Executive Officer, 49 Links Road, Ardross 6153, Australia.
Tel: +61 8 9364 3553.

Austria   Verband der Tanzlehrer Österreichs, Mr Otto Huber,
President, Nikolaigasse 4, 9500 Villach, Austria.
Tel: +43 4242 28073.

Belarus   Belarus Professional Dance Union, Mr Vassily
Lyashenko, President, 15, 46-"B" 15 Fr. Scorina Avenue,
Minsk 220005, Belarus. Tel: +375 172 848479.

Belgium   Belgische Unie van Leraren in Danse en
Omgangvoren (BULDO), Mr Guido De Smet, President,
St Benedictusstraat 2, 3020 Herent, Belgium. Tel: +32 16 488022
+32 16 206663.

Canada   Canadian Dance Teachers' Association, Mrs Patricia
Nikleva, National Ballroom Consultant, 8160 Lucas Road,
Richmond V6Y IG3, Canada. Tel: +1 604 277 6480;
+1 604 277 4144.

Chinese Taipei   Chinese Taipei Council of Ballroom Dancing,
Mr David Lee, President, 4th FL 94 Chung Hsiao E.Rd Sec 4,
Taipei, Chinese Taipei. Tel: +886 22 7772177; +886 224 7810949.

Czech Republic   Asociace Profesionalniho Tance (PDA), Mr
Jiri Kopecný, Dance Sport Board, Elisky Krásnohorské 11
Praha 1, Prague 110 00, Czech Republic. Tel: +420 2232 6489;
+420 2 21596258.

Denmark   Danselærer Organisationernes Forening (DOF),
Mr Jørgen Christensen, President, Fredericksvaerkgade 43A,
3400 Hillerød DK-3400, Denmark. Tel: +45 48 26 5709.

Estonia   Estonian Association of Teachers of Dancing, Mr Janek
Randla, President, Aardla 156-4, Tartu 50415, Estonia.
Tel: +372 7 428292.

Finland   The Finnish Association of Teachers of Dancing,
Mr Jarmo Nuutinen, President, Isonpuuntie 1, Espoo 02920,
Finland. Tel: +358 9 8537072.

France   Conseil Français Professionel de Danse Social, Mr René
Barsi, Président, 22 rue Victor Hugo, Montreuil 93 100, France.
Tel: +33 1 48 59 21 24.

Georgia   Georgian League of Dance and Sport Dance,
Mr Roman Archaya, President, 121-4/15 Tsinamzgvrishvili Str.,
Tbilisi 380 000, Georgia. Tel: +995 32 943856.

Germany   Allegemeiner Deutscher Tanzlehrer Verband,
Mr Heiko Feltens, Präsident, Mönchengang 7–9, Dortmund
D-44135, Germany. Tel: +49 231 524444.

Great Britain   British Dance Council, Mr Dane Edwards,
Company Secretary, Terpsichore House, 240 Merton Road
South, Wimbledon, London SW19 1EQ, Great Britain.
Tel: +44 181 545 0085.

Scottish Dance Teachers' Alliance, Mr Johnny Stewart,
6 Richmond Drive, Bishopbriggs, Glasgow G64 3HR,
Great Britain. Tel: +44 141 772 5539.

Greece   National Dance Council of Greece, Mr Dimitrios
Caravas, General Secretary, 27th Lagoumitzi Str., Kallithea,
Athens 17671, Greece. Tel: +33 01 922 3082; +33 01 9234464.

Holland   Federatie Dansleraren Organisaties (FDO-PR), FDO
Secretariat, J B weg 6, 7991 RG Dwingeloo, Holland.
Tel: +31 52159 2071.

Hong Kong   Hong Kong Ballroom Dancing Council, Mr Walter
Wat, President, PO Box 25562, Harbour Building, Central
Hong Kong. Tel: +852 2541 6215; +852 2541 6105.

Hungary Council of Hungarian Dance Teachers and Professionals, Mr Attila Becz, President, 1112 Budapest Menyecske u. 27, Hungary. Tel: +36 1 3101 106.

Iceland Dansrað Islands, Official Board of Dancing, Iceland, Mr Heidar R'Astvaldsson, President, Box 5048, Reykjavik, Iceland. Tel: +354 553 8126.

Indonesia Indonesian Council of Ballroom Dancing, Dr Ken Ariata Tengadi, Executive Secretary, Jalan Taman Sari X no. 32, Jakarta 10340, Indonesia. Tel: +62 21 659 4988.

Ireland All Ireland Board of Ballroom Dancing, Mr George Devlin, Pine Ridge, Kilmacanogue, Co. Wicklow, Ireland. Tel: +353 1 286 1678(o); +353 1 286 8101(h).

Israel Israel Association of Teachers and Professional Dancers, Mr Anatoly Trilisky, President, POB 6139, Kiryat Eqron 70500, Israel. Tel: +972 8 941 14 76.

Italy Consiglio Italiano Danza Sportiva, Mr Enrico Maggioni, General Secretary, Via Monteverdi 9, Trezzano S/N 20090, Italy. Tel: +39 0 2 4452140; +39 0 2 8435409.

Japan Japan Dance Council, Mr Edward Kibata, Liaison Officer, 1888-4 Minami-Kaname, Hiratsuka City, Kanagawa-Pref, 259-12, Japan. Tel: +81 463 58 8847.

Korea (South) Korean National Council of Ballroom Dancing, Mr Geoffrey S Chun, Vice President, #405, E Sak B/D, 63, Young Dung Po 5-Ga, Young Dung Po-Gu, Seoul 150-035, Korea (South). Tel: +82 2 671 4823; +82 2 785 3225.

Latvia Latvijas Sporta deju Professionalu Federacija, Mr Egils Smagris, President, Gertrudes iela 42-9, Riga LV-1011, Latvia. Tel: +371 34 23370.

Lithuania Union of Lithuanian Sport Dance Professionals, Mrs Olga Gunko, President, A. Baranausko Str. 19 A-12, Kaunas 3028, Lithuania. Tel: +370 7 794 333; +370 7 380 209.

Luxembourg Luxembourg Dance & Dance Sport Council, Miss Rita Emeringer, 2, op Raechels, L-4702, Luxembourg. Tel: +352 509535; +352 779137.

Malaysia   Malaysian Dancers' Association, Dr Henry Kwee Lim Ooi, KMN President, Chateau Gay, 119 York Road, Penang 10450, Malaysia. Tel: +60 4 261 6495; +60 4 226 3807(h).

Malta   Malta Dance & Dance Sport Council, Ms Carmen Baldacchino, Chairperson, Peacock Buildings, No. 101 Testaferrata Street, Msida, MSD 02, Malta. Tel: +356 312806.

Moldova   Moldova Professional Dance Sport Association, Ms Svetlana Gozun, President, C/P 1856 Str. P. Movila, 41, Kishnev, Y 2004, Moldova. Tel: +373 276 6468; +373 224 8761.

New Zealand   New Zealand Dance & Dancesport Council, Mrs Sherrall Macown, Secretary, PO Box 37-342 Parnell, Auckland, New Zealand. Tel: +64 9 528 0065.

Norway   Norges Danselærer Forbund, c/o Norges Danseforbund, Norwegian Dance Federation, Hauger Skolevei 1 1351 RUD, Norway. Tel: +47 67 154600; +47 67 154709.

Philippines   Professional Dance Teachers Association of the Philippines, Ms Maribel Dario, Chairman, c/o PRISM Rm. 502 5/F TLRC Bldg., Makati City, Philippines. Tel: +632 895 8184; +632 895 2021.

Poland   Polish Professional Dance Association, Mr Krzysztof Wasilewski, President, A1. Pilsudskiego 54 A, Olsztyn 10-577, Poland. Tel: +48 89 5 349 404.

Portugal   Associação Portuguesa De Professores De Dança De Salão Internacional, Mr Toni Pinto, President, Apartado 78, 2766 São João Do, Estoril, Portugal. Tel: +351 1 468 0449.

Russia   Russian Dance Union, Mr Stanislav Popov, President, Novatorov Str 26-52, Moscow 117421, Russia. Tel: +7 095 432 3229.

Singapore   Singapore Ballroom Dance Teachers' Association, Mr Sunny Low, President, 263 Outram Road, 0316, Singapore. Tel: +65 278 1502.

Slovakia   Slovak Dance Association, Mr Igor Jagersky, President, STZ-Slovenský Tanecný Zváz JUNÁCKA 6, SK 832 80 Bratislava, Slovakia. Tel: +421 7 368 208; +421 7 3846 203.

Slovenia Slovene Professional Dance Organization (ZPVUT), Mr Miran Pritekelj, Secretary, PP 2507, 1001 Ljubljana, Slovenia. Tel: +386 61 15 21 643; +386 61 15 81 284.

South Africa South African National Council of Ballroom Dancing (SANCBD), Mrs Jessie Liddell, Secretary, PO Box 446, Kloof Kwa Zulu, Natal 3640, South Africa. Tel: +27 31 207 5663.

Spain Asociacion Espanola de Professores de Bailes de Salon, Mr Ferran Rovira, President, Torrent de l'Olla 16-18, 1-3, 08012 Barcelona, Spain. Tel: +34 93 457 25 48.

Sweden Sveriges Danspedagogers Riksförbund, Mr Egon Dernell, General Secretary, Box 193, SE-125 25 Älvsjö, Sweden. Tel: +46 8 99 09 15.

Switzerland Swiss Dance, Mr Viktor Berger, President, Eichtalhoehe 8, CH-5400 Baden, Switzerland. Tel: +41 56 221 6262; +41 56 221 2381.

Thailand Thailand Association of Teachers of Dancing, Mr Boonlert Krabuansaeng, President, 212/31-32, Sukhumvit Plaza, 4th Floor Soi 12, Sukhumvit Road, Klongtoey, Bangkok 10110, Thailand. Tel: +66 2 653 3979.

Ukraine Ukrainian Dance Board, Ms Irena Bous', President, Box 9040, Lviv 290011, Ukraine. Tel: +380 322 72 2636.

USA National Dance Council of America, Mr Brian McDonald, President, PO Box 490, San Juan, Capistrano, 92693, USA. Tel: +1 949 728 0348.

Yugoslavia Yugoslav Dance Teachers Association UPVUTJ, Mr Dragan Radovanovic, President, Sjenicka 1, 11000 Beogrand, Yugoslavia. Tel: +381 11 4887 483.